Rhododendrons

PETER A. COX

LONDON

The Royal Horticultural Society

Revised 1977

Contents

Line drawings: Jill Cox

Rhododendrons

1. The genus Rhododendron

There are few gardens in Britain where at least one or two rhododendrons cannot be grown successfully. Provided that some simple cultural practices are carried out there can be hardly any shrub that gives greater reward for less attention. In favourable localities and in a year of little frost many gardens can have rhododendrons in flower for every month of the year.

To most people the word rhododendron is associated with a medium-sized bush with dark green, shiny evergreen leaves and mauve, pink or red flowers. Only two names are well known, the common *R. ponticum* which has naturalised itself over large areas of Britain, and the hybrid 'Pink Pearl' which still remains about the most popular variety. Few realise that the genus includes nearly 1000 species (as found in the wild) and many thousands of hybrids (crosses between either two species or subsequent crossings). These range from dwarf creeping alpines only an inch or two high, to trees of up to 80 feet often with single trunks. The leaves may vary from $\frac{1}{4}$ inch (0.6 cm) to about 2 feet (60 cm) long, and the flower colours range from near blue to violet, crimson, red, orange, yellow and white, with many combinations and intermediates of these colours.

Azaleas are included botanically in this great genus. They are divided into several groups, the chief of which are the commonly evergreen or semi-evergreen, so-called Japanese, azaleas, which include the familiar indoor pot plants. These all belong to one section of the genus known as the Obtusum subseries of the Azalea Series and will hereafter be referred to as Obtusum azaleas. The other main group contains almost entirely deciduous species. Here belong the well known *R. luteum* (*"Azalea pontica"*) and the Mollis and Exbury hybrids.

The rest of the genus is also divided into series and subseries which affords a convenient method of grouping the species with similarity in botanical characters.

A feature, common in several series, is the presence of a soft felt-like covering, generally on the undersides of the leaves, which is known as "indumentum".

Species may vary in the wild. If an extreme variation remains constant, it may be given a varietal name in Latin such as *R. glaucophyllum* var. *luteiflorum*. A seedling of a species which has been raised in cultivation, may prove to be of special merit and be given what is known as a cultivar or clonal name. An example is *R. calostrotum* 'Gigha'. To multiply a clone, it must be propagated vegetatively only (that is from cuttings, layers or grafts). Seedlings do not have exactly the same characters as the parents. **Hybrids.** In the past all the progeny of one cross were often given a collective name known to botanists as a grex name. This led to the distribution under one name, for instance Loderi, of the various seedlings of the particular cross, whether they were good, bad or indifferent. If a seedling was picked out as being of special merit, there was no means of distinguishing it by name from its (possibly inferior) sisters. Now each selected seedling must be named, so that it has both a grex name, which it shares with its sisters, and a clonal or cultivar name of its own. For example Rhododendron Loderi (a cross between *R. fortunei* and *R. griffithianum*) includes several selected seedlings, i.e. 'Loderi King George', 'Loderi Pink Diamond', 'Loderi Venus' and others.

2. Rhododendrons in the Wild

2.1. Where they grow naturally

The huge genus Rhododendron, one of the largest in the plant kingdom, grows naturally over large areas of rain-soaked mountains, almost entirely in the northern hemisphere. Although a few species are sub-tropical and come from damp jungles, the vast majority grow high up in the mountains in the temperate zone, sometimes not far below the snow line.

The species can be divided roughly into two groups, those that come from the sub-tropics or further north, where distinct summer and winter seasons occur, and those from near the equator, where there is no proper winter resting period. This difference is very important from a garden point of view. The first group come from a climate fairly similar to our own in Britain, and it is these species and their hybrids which we can grow successfully out-of-doors. The second group cannot endure our cold winters and therefore have to be grown in cool greenhouses. The latter species come mainly from the islands of New Guinea, Borneo, Sumatra and Java and are known as the Malesian rhododendrons.

Unfortunately, not all those species from the temperate regions are hardy throughout Britain. Only those which live naturally in conditions like our own can be grown satisfactorily. Generally speaking, the higher up the mountains they are found, the hardier they are. The great majority of these temperate species come from the eastern Himalaya, north-east Burma and north-west China, with outliers in Japan, north-east Asia, Turkey and the Caucasus, Europe and north America.

The altitude at which they grow depends on latitude. Species in Europe and Turkey, Japan and north America, may grow from sea level up to 9,000 ft., (2743 m.) whereas those in the Himalaya and north-west China are mostly found between 5,000 to 16,000 ft. (1522-4875 m). Surprisingly enough, the species we find the hardiest in this country are not those from the high Himalayan altitudes, but those from the much lower mountains in Japan, Turkey and north America. Most of our garden hybrids of today are derived from crossing the latter hardier species with the more tender ones from mainland Asia.

2.2. Why are they found there?
Generally speaking, all rhododendrons like similar conditions of soil and of climate. In the temperate regions where they are found wild, there is nearly always an abundance of summer rains or a mist, relatively cool summers and a soil rich in organic matter. This organic matter has built up in conditions where the breakdown of fallen leaves and the rotting of branches as well as herbaceous plant materials is slow.

Rhododendrons and their relations, the heathers, vacciniums, and others, are highly successful colonisers of this type of habitat. All produce great quantities of seed which generally germinate rapidly in warm, moist situations. The ideal, natural seedbed for rhododendrons is moss and it so happens that mosses like a similar habitat.

Rhododendrons in the wild are found growing happily in a great many different situations; the tops of trees, cliff ledges, on and amongst boulders, by waterfalls, on rocks in a river, on moorlands and pasture, amongst bamboo, in bogs and in many types of forest. The same species are not seen in all these places, but they could be found in several of them. This shows that, given the right climate, rhododendrons are very versatile indeed.

All species in nature demand perfect drainage. Even those growing on so-called bogs usually sit up on tufts and are given a periodic partial drying out in autumn and winter. Alpine rhododendrons from the Himalayas and north-west China are protected from the icy blasts that sweep over these mountains in winter, by heavy snow falls. When uncovered by snow in low temperatures, most rhododendrons curl up their leaves to cut down moisture loss. Under a snow cover, the temperature remains surprisingly even and the loss of water from transpiration is very little.

Unfortunately, in Britain we cannot be sure of a snow covering and frequently our worst frosts and cold winds occur when the ground is bare, causing damage to the unprotected plants. In the wild, every advantage is taken of any shelter available from rocks and boulders and hollows, at high altitudes. The same applies to shade, especially in the heavy monsoon areas, where mist and rain prevail throughout the growing season. Here we may have several weeks of hot sunny weather. It might be said that prolonged spells of sunshine are rare, but when they do come they can take their toll especially of anything newly planted. Those species, which grow naturally in full exposure in the drier parts of north-west China, can take and enjoy nearly full sun in any part of Britain, but most others appreciate a little shade at least during the hottest part of the day.

Rhododendrons are notorious for their dislike of lime, and yet certain species have been found in nature growing on limestone. But even in these conditions, little free calcium occurs in the soil although the soil may be alkaline. This alkalinity is normally induced by magnesium. It is true though that those species found growing naturally on limestone are the ones that are most tolerant of lime in cultivation and this tolerance has been passed on to many of their hybrids. Certain rhododendrons can be grown satisfactorily in a neutral soil.

Some of these will be found in Chapter 9.

3. Preparing for Planting

3.1. Finding a site

In these days of small suburban houses, few people have much choice of site for their gardening, although many have a plot both in front of and behind the house, giving at least a different exposure to the elements. Those with an acre or two of garden will probably have a few established trees, and in time it might be possible to create both a woodland garden and a rock or peat garden. The combination of these two types of garden enables one to grow successfully a very large range of rhododendrons.

Before planting rhododendrons, there are a few basic factors which must be considered. Firstly, the existing soil and its drainage. If it is a heavy clay, or at all alkaline, it is no use expecting to grow rhododendrons planted directly into this soil. Beware of beds near walls which may contain lime. With the use of carefully constructed raised beds (see page 8) a collection of small varieties may be grown successfully. With adequate preparation lighter soils of an acid nature should grow rhododendrons well, provided a little shelter and shade is given and atmospheric pollution is not chronic. If it is, it is better to grow a collection of dwarf varieties in a greenhouse.

In a larger garden, where there is a choice of site, avoid hollows where frost might collect. Frost tends to flow like water and gather at the lowest points. Try to avoid positions where early flowering varieties will catch the early morning sun. It is astonishing how even a few yards can make all the difference between complete destruction of the flowers by frost, and no damage at all.

In seaside districts, protection may have to be given against salt spray, which, if severe, can defoliate certain varieties.

For those who garden in heavy rainfall areas, usually near the milder west coast, try planting the tender species (which grow naturally on trees or rocks) on mossy tree stumps and trunks or on mossy rocks. Perched up above ground level, they make fascinating focal points of interest. Tender varieties can often be grown successfully against a shady wall, especially in the corner of two walls.

3.2. Improving the Environment
Shade. As a general rule, the larger the leaf, the more shade is required, although, of course, there are exceptions. Plants in the sunnier drier parts of the country require the most shade.

For giving shade, oak and Scots pine are amongst the best trees. The oak is especially good as the roots are mostly deep in the soil with the shallow roots of the rhododendron above. Beech, together with oak, produces excellent leaf-mould for mulching and feeding, but the beeches cast too deep a shade to plant underneath. Other trees to avoid, where possible, are ash, elm and birch, which have shallow, greedy root systems. Sycamore casts a heavy shade, drops honey-dew from the aphids feeding on the leaves, which then go black with sooty mould and the seedlings come up by the thousand everywhere.

The majority of small-leaved maples, cherries, and species of *Sorbus*, *Styrax*, *Halesia*, *Cornus*, and others, make excellent smaller shade trees.
Shelter. In small gardens, shelter is often already provided by walls, buildings and hedges, although of course a new building site may be exposed. It is much better, in most circumstances, to try to reduce the velocity of the wind by a permeable barrier, such as a wattle fence, a beech hedge or a narrow belt of trees. Solid walls and shelter belts of close growing conifers tend only to alter the direction of the wind, which often comes around corners or hits the ground again, some yards further on, just as hard as when it hit the barrier. The taller the hedge or shelter belt, the longer the distance behind it which it will shelter. One of the finest tall hedging plants now available is × *Cupressocyparis leylandii*, which does not become too wide and grows very fast. Beech is excellent but slow. *Chamaecyparis lawsoniana* is good, but rather solid.

For coastal areas, sycamore and Sitka spruce stand up well to the blast, as do *Pinus contorta* and *Pinus radiata* and Corsican and Austrian pines. For warmer coastal districts, excellent secondary breaks can be provided by *Griselinia littoralis*, *Elaeagnus* varieties, *Olearia albida*, *O. macrodonta*, *O. travesii* and *Escallonia macrantha* and the larger hybrids.
Plants to associate with rhododendrons. In nature, nearly all rhododendrons are social plants and grow in large colonies, either all one species, or up to several mixed together, sometimes to the exclusion of other genera. In other cases, they may grow in clumps between trees, in a pasture and among other shrubs, or, more rarely, associated with herbaceous plants.

The chief feeding area of rhododendrons is just below the surface of the soil and therefore any other plants growing over the roots compete with them for food and water. Many people advocate planting herbaceous plants along with rhododendrons, but for the reason given above, they are wrong. Well grown rhododendrons should have branches right down to the ground wherever possible. Not only are the roots then shaded by the plant's own foliage, which is beneficial, but the lower branches trap falling leaves which help to mulch and feed naturally. By all means, plant groups of woodland-loving plants in clumps between the rhododendrons, but never *over* their root systems. Plants which associate well under these conditions are related ericaceous shrubs, such as *Vaccinium*, *Gaultheria*, *Phyllodoce*, *Cassiope* species and the larger growing *Pieris* and *Enkianthus*. Then in suitable situations groups of primulas, meconopsis and gentians, lilies, trilliums and erythroniums can be planted.

Dwarf rhododendrons, especially, should be grown socially. Careful grouping of the different leaf colours will maintain an interest even when the plants are not in flower, and it is important to grade the heights, the taller varieties to the back of a border with the lower growing dwarfs planted to give an undulating effect towards the front.

3.3. Preparation of the soil

The longer one grows rhododendrons the more one realises that it always pays to prepare the ground adequately beforehand. 'Adequately' means providing conditions in which the roots of rhododendrons can grow happily.

There are two methods of preparation: either dig individual holes, or make a bed to take several plants. If the ground is not naturally full of organic matter and is already loose and friable, as large an area as possible should be prepared for each plant. In other words, prepare enough ground to allow for many years expansion of the root system. Beds, of course, are the best, but there is not always enough room for them.

Attention has been drawn earlier to the necessity for perfect drainage. Under all soil conditions but the heaviest clays, drainage can be carried out, either by laying tiles or digging open ditches. If the ground is pure peat, tiles are not very satisfactory. But if the soil is a heavy clay or is limey, it is essential to make raised beds. These are now used very successfully in many parts of the United States of America. There, either a 100% new soil mixture is added above the existing soil level and held in position by boards, or about 30% of the top soil is incorporated with organic materials and very well mixed into a more friable mixture. Coarse sawdust is ideal, mixed with nitrogen to aid the breakdown and to avoid nitrogen starvation of the plants, but in Britain this type of sawdust is rarely available. A combination of all or some of the following should give good results: sandy soil, oak or beech leaf-mould, spruce or pine needles, forest litter, wood chips, shredded bark, rotten wood, bracken litter, hop manure and fibrous or coarse peat moss. Sawdust and shredded bark should have ammonium sulphate added, at the rate of 12 lbs. per 1000 sq. ft. for every inch (2.5 cm) applied.

For individual holes, the quantity of peat (bagged or baled moss or fibrous) and leaf-mould to be added depends on the amount of organic matter already present in the soil. Where organic matter is lacking, fork over the base of the hole, then add at least two large full shovels each of peat and leaf-mould and mix well in. Break up the edge of the hole where it meets the hard ground so as not to leave a sudden division between made up ground and undug soil.

Similarly, beds lacking in organic matter should have at least three inches of peat and leaf-mould spread on them and this should be very well forked in with any clods broken up. Although almost any peat is better than none, ideally, coarse fibrous peat is best, either sedge or sphagnum. The leaf-mould should be beech or oak or a combination of the two, only from trees grown on acid soil. It has been proved that leaf-mould collected from chalk or limey areas is alkaline and therefore unsuitable for rhododendrons.

For alpine varieties, peat beds are ideal, built up on terraces made with peat blocks. The blocks should be as large and even as possible and they are better set in position when they are damp, as when really dry they take a long time to swell and then distort the line of the wall. Soak them if necessary. The walls are better when not more than three or four blocks high, laid like bricks, but slanted inwards and well packed with soil both behind and under the blocks. Wire pegs help to keep them in place. Prepare the actual beds as described above. A few small plants can be inserted in the wall, between the blocks.

Only large growing rhododendrons should be planted in individual holes. All azaleas and dwarf rhododendrons appreciate beds much better and will be kept free of weeds more easily.

3.4. In the greenhouse and in the house
Many different rhododendrons and azaleas may be grown indoors, either in pots or in other containers which can be brought into the house, or planted in beds in the greenhouse. Most of those are grown indoors because they are tender, but certain hardy Obtusum azaleas do well inside and now certain hybrid rhododendrons are being forced by combinations of specially regulated day-lengths and chemical growth controllers. It may be a few years before we see many of these forced rhododendrons in this country.

The ordinary indoor azaleas are nearly all grown in Belgium and exported from Holland to Britain to force into flower during the winter.

If well looked after, that is, repotted and properly watered and fed, there is no reason why these azaleas should not last for years and grow into fine specimens. For those with no greenhouse, keep them well watered until flowering has finished and then repot, using a good soilless compost. John Innes potting mixture would be too far removed from the original peat, and the plant will have difficulty rooting into a mixture different to that to which it was accustomed. Use the recommended fertilizers without chalk. Never allow the root ball to dry out at any time.

Many of the scented rhododendrons do well indoors. Nearly all are too tender to survive outside in any but the mildest coastal areas. The flowers are white tinged with pink and some have the most delicious scent, a joy in the house in the early spring.

Another group that is excellent indoors are the early species, such as *R. leucaspis* and *R. moupinense* and hybrids like 'Cilpinense', often growing a better shape than the scented varieties. These are mostly pink, yellow or white and free flowering from February to March with very little forcing. In fact if they are forced too much, some flower colour and size is lost.

During the summer, all these varieties in pots, including the azaleas, should be plunged in soil or ashes outside after the danger of frost is over, in a relatively shady position, say at the foot of a north-facing wall or hedge. Keep well watered in dry weather and bring indoors again in autumn before any frost occurs. If there is no greenhouse, place by a window in a coolish room and again remember to keep damp. If there is a greenhouse but no heat, plunge the pots up to the rims and keep well ventilated in all but cold frosty weather. If some heat is possible, set the temperature at 40°F or lower until at least February, when the buds start swelling and the heat can be raised a little. Some azaleas, if given extra heat, will open for Christmas. Keep the house well ventilated unless the weather is cold. Many of these plants are likely to drop their buds if the temperature goes too high or the pots dry out. Naturally, severe frost will damage the buds of the more tender varieties and all are susceptible once the buds begin to swell. In spring and early summer, keep the greenhouse well damped down in sunny weather.

Many potted azaleas or rhododendrons may become leggy or spread too much. Unfortunately most of the scented kinds are inclined to sprawl and produce few branches. Pinching out the growth buds may induce more branching, or the longest shoots may be cut back to where there is a bud or shorter growth. 'Fragrantissimum' is sometimes tied in all round to produce a "basket" effect.

In the greenhouse, beds should have at least 1 foot (30 cm) of soil with perfect drainage underneath. An ideal mixture is $\frac{1}{3}$ sandy acid soil, $\frac{1}{3}$ peat and $\frac{1}{3}$ oak or beech leaf-mould.

Another use for the greenhouse or frames, is for dwarf rhododendrons, either for the show bench, to protect plants from atmospheric pollution or when avoiding alkaline soil. They may be grown indoors throughout the year. Square wooden boxes dry out less than pots and are best made of teak. Leave a space at the top of the pot or box of $1\frac{1}{2}$ to 2 inches (3·8 to 5 cm) to allow for a top dressing and repot every two years. Cut back if necessary immediately after flowering. Either soilless or John Innes potting compost may be used, without chalk, possibly with the addition of oak or beech leaf-mould. If the water is a little hard, add $\frac{1}{2}$ oz. of ferrous sulphate per gallon, but if very hard, use only rain water.

4. Where and how to plant

4.1. What time of year?

One of the excellent characters of rhododendrons, including azaleas, is that they are easy to move, even when quite large, providing they can be man-handled.

It is possible to move rhododendrons throughout the year. But anything transplanted in late spring and summer will need extra care over watering and shading. One advantage of moving when in flower is that a colour scheme can be rearranged while it can be seen what is wanted.

Early autumn is the ideal time to plant. The roots get a chance to settle in before winter and then the winter snow and rains bed the plant in thoroughly before spring. Late autumn planting is quite satisfactory and so is planting in early spring, but the danger in spring is the dry east wind which can desiccate a plant before it is established, so care should be taken over extra watering and shelter. Do not plant into frozen ground.

One disadvantage often overlooked comes with buying rhododendrons from a nursery in an earlier locality than one's own. Even in Scotland, there may be at least two weeks' difference between a low sheltered garden facing south and a cold exposed garden at 1,000 ft. above sea level. A plant transferred from the low area to the high, in spring, could be a full two weeks ahead of what it would have been had it been transferred in the autumn, making it far more susceptible to a cold spring spell.

Garden centres are now found all over the country and a higher and higher proportion of plants are being sold from these. Many are purchased in some type of container when in flower, for planting direct into the garden. This is an excellent idea because one knows exactly what is being bought, but these plants often take longer to establish and will need more care over watering for the rest of their first season.

Do not be surprised if a well-budded specimen does not flower again for a year to two. Several nurserymen prepare their plants to be well budded the year they are sold and then the plants take a year or two to recover and grow away again. Many of the larger varieties are better if bought without flower buds. It is far better to sacrifice flowers at an early age for growth, and thus end up with a much finer specimen plant.

With modern methods of rooting cuttings, it should no longer be necessary to propagate by grafting, except for a few difficult varieties. So many rhododendrons grafted on to *R. ponticum* are ultimately ruined by the rootstock growing away. If grafting is really necessary, it should be done on either species or varieties that do not sucker readily.

Many species are hard to propagate from cuttings and are uneconomic to layer. Named clonal varieties of these species are often very hard to find and are expensive. By hand pollinating, using two good forms of a species, relatively cheap seedlings may be produced in quantity and these are excellent value, nearly all proving as good if not better than their parents. Species from wild collected seed are rare these days with so much of Asia closed to collectors. These are always great fun to have, especially if it is known exactly where the seed originated, and may be particularly good forms.

For those people who want instant rhododendrons, large plants can be bought but they are relatively expensive and do not always make such fine specimens as those grown on from the normal size available. These plants generally have to have quite a proportion of their root system and/or the soil ball, removed for transport and therefore require considerable care for the first year or two, before becoming established.

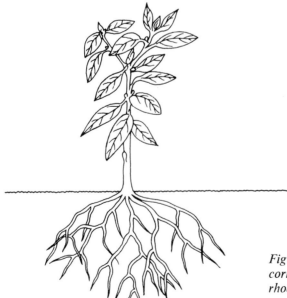

Fig. 1. The normal correct planting level for rhododendrons

12

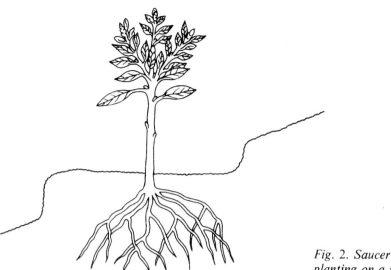

*Fig. 2. Saucer
planting on a slope*

4.2. How to plant correctly

Never plant a rhododendron too deeply. Only a bare sprinkling of soil should be put on top of the root ball and it is usually simple to find the mark of the old soil-level near the base of the stem. Space out any loose roots at their proper level and push soil gently underneath them. The one exception to this method is with young grafted plants. These should be placed a little deeper each time they are moved so that the scion (above the graft union) can form roots itself. Never mound up soil around the stem after planting. Never tramp in too firmly, especially in heavy soil, because rhododendrons like well aerated soil conditions. It is a good idea to water in well after planting with a hose or coarse rose on a watering can.

It is sometimes necessary to firm a rather top-heavy plant around the neck, but staking is usually needed as well. If possible, push or knock in the stake before planting and tie securely with fibre string or raffia, not wire or plastic string which may eat into the stem if left on too long.

On a very light, well drained soil, especially on a slope, planting in a "saucer" is beneficial. Not only does it conserve moisture, but also leaves a place to hold a mulch. Never plant on a mound when the soil is liable to dry out. Only where the rainfall is very heavy or the drainage imperfect are mounds advisable.

The distance to plant is a matter of choice, whether an immediate effect is desired or a few years may be taken to close the gaps. Dwarfs and Obtusum azaleas are relatively small and can easily be transplanted when they become crowded, but the larger varieties are more difficult owing to their size and the weight of the root ball. It is always better to give too much,

13

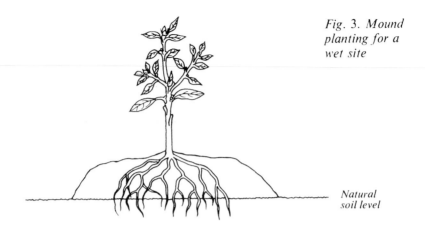

Fig. 3. Mound planting for a wet site

Natural
soil level

rather than too little room. Really well spaced out bushes, with branches down to ground level and enough space to walk round them are infinitely preferable to lanky overcrowded specimens reaching for the sky, where one strains one's neck to see the flowers! Of course it takes a long time to reach this state of affairs, but do look to the future when planting. A good idea is to plant 3 or more of one variety close together as rhododendrons are naturally communal plants.

5. Regular Care

5.1. Mulches, manures and lime

Mulches. A mulch is a layer of organic matter applied to the surface of the soil. It serves various purposes: (1) To retain moisture. (2) To control weeds. (3) To provide organic matter as a nutrient. (4) To modify the surface temperature of the soil. (5) To prevent erosion by rain. (6) To reduce the depth to which frost reaches in the ground. In climates with hot summers and cold winters, all these points are of importance, but in Britain, (1), (2) and (3) are of the most significance.

Good mulches to use here are oak and beech leaf-mould, pine and spruce needles; and chopped or pulverised fresh bracken fronds. Hop manure is another alternative. Sawdust is only really good if coarse; few saws used in this country produce this grade, because the teeth are not large enough. Fine sawdust tends to mat down too much and form a cake. Micro-organisms take nitrogen from the soil for the breakdown of wood by-products, robbing the plants of nitrogen underneath. Therefore extra nitrogen must be added as ammonium sulphate. This should be applied at approximately 12 lbs. per 1000 sq. ft. (93 sq. m.) of surface for every inch depth of sawdust put on. Some gardeners give several light applications of fertilizer instead of one heavy one. Excellent partially decomposed shredded bark is now available which does not require added nitrogen.

Rough peat is a good mulch but dries out too much in hot, dry weather and then becomes hard to wet again. It also tends to encourage too many surface roots which are easily damaged by drought and frost.

Unsuitable mulches. Really unsuitable mulches are grass cuttings which become a horrid, soggy mat; and leaf-mould either from alkaline soil or from such trees as elm, sycamore, lime and horse chestnut. These break down to give an alkaline reaction and have a powdery texture, both being undesirable for rhododendrons. Straw and hay are messy, blow away and hay seeds add to the weeds.

To be successful for suppressing weeds and conserving moisture, a mulch should be at least 3 inches deep. The easiest way to supply a rhododendron with a mulch of leaves, is to put any prunings of dead wood, fallen branches, or twigs, around the root area of big, established bushes. This may be considered a little unsightly by some people. All large branches can be cut or broken into smaller bits. These trap the leaves when they fall where they are wanted over the rhododendron roots, instead of being blown away. Never collect and burn leaves among these plants; even the poorer leaf types mentioned above are better than none.

Manures. Various concentrated fertilizers, both organic and inorganic can be used on the majority of rhododendrons *in moderation*, but they are *no* substitute for organic matter. If a compound of ready mixed fertilizer is used, it should contain a relatively small amount of nitrogen, in ammonium form if possible. Most fertilizers are sold with an analysis giving the nitrogen, phosphorus and potassium content, using the abbreviations, N.P.K. For use in the spring, a mixture of 5 parts N to 10 P and 10 K is ideal applied at 1 oz. per sq. yd.

Rhododendrons and azaleas that are happy, that is, have healthy foliage, adequate growth and when mature enough, flower freely, should not be given fertilizers and manures. With an abundance of good leaf mould and a suitable soil underneath plants rarely need extra feeding. But in many cases, especially on light, peaty or hungry soils, these materials can be beneficial.

The varieties that respond best are the deciduous hybrid azaleas of the Exbury, Mollis and Ghent types, also some of the so-called hardy hybrid rhododendrons such as 'Pink Pearl' and 'Purple Splendour'. Many others, especially those related to *R. neriiflorum* are very susceptible to doses of nitrogen and get leaf scorch very easily.

Nitrogen is of value for inducing growth and healthy foliage. Phosphate and potassium help the ripening of wood and the formation of flower

15

buds. Many other elements are also essential for the well-being of a plant. Magnesium for photosynthesis (formation of chlorophyll in the leaf) and sulphur and calcium in small quantities are also necessary. The trace elements, likewise, must also be available. Luckily all are usually present in the average soil in sufficient quantities, but if not, there are various compound fertilizers and liquid feeds which now contain all the elements.

Several slow acting compounds now available are excellent for trees and shrubs. In very small quantities, organic manures, such as bone meal, hoof and horn, and fish meal are suitable. Bone meal contains a minute amount of lime, but this is so small it does not harm rhododendrons.

Beware of all farmyard manures. Any used should be really well rotted. Cow manure is sometimes used, but is not as good as leaf-mould or needles. Hen manure has led to disasters from excess ammonia. The golden rule is, always use fertilizers and manures in moderation and follow instructions carefully. Better to be safe than sorry.

Lime. Much has been written on the subject of limey and chalky soils, in relation to rhododendrons. If excess calcium is present in the soil, rhododendrons take up too much of it and poison themselves. Soils in which they grow naturally are low in calcium and rhododendrons are very efficient in utilising any that is available.

The whole question of soils and the elements contained therein, is very complex, which cannot be explained here. Not only are rhododendrons poisoned by lime, but excessive quantities lock up other elements present in such a way that the plants cannot use them. The result is usually severe chlorosis and frequently death. There is no easy way of growing rhododendrons on lime or chalk soils. Raised beds have been mentioned on p. 8. Another suggestion is to line holes with flowers of sulphur and fill with rotted bracken and acid peat which are also mixed with the soil at the edge of the hole. Then mulch with pine needles and chopped bracken, every year. Some rhododendrons have grown well this way for years.

Various chemical compounds are available for helping rhododendrons to grow in unsuitable soils: these are chelates and fritted trace elements. While they are of some value in improving the colour of foliage and the general health of rhododendrons, the former is liable to cause severe scorch and death even if the instructions are carried out carefully. These chemicals make the various trace elements, such as iron and manganese, available to the plants. It is said that rhododendrons are more easily grown on limestone than on pure chalk. See chapter 9 for the most lime tolerant species.

5.2. Watering

Many sheltered woodland gardens with a heavy rainfall and a soil rich in organic matter, rarely if ever really suffer from drought, once rhododendrons are fully established. But many of us are not so lucky. In an average summer there may be one or two periods when conditions get really dry, with perhaps three weeks without measurable rain. If one of these droughts occurs during the main growing season from April to July, it can be serious, and if no watering is done, plants can suffer especially in the first season or two after planting. Plants which have been well mulched are less susceptible to drought, because the layer of organic matter on the soil surface prevents some loss of water.

In a large garden there are always certain areas which dry out first. This may be because of too much sun, shallow soil, overhead trees or tree roots. Any bush in full growth will need special attention at these times.

When watering always give a really good soak. A sprinkler can be left on for at least $1\frac{1}{2}$ hours, but soil conditions and the type of equipment used must be considered when deciding the length of time to water. The snag comes during the rare, really prolonged drought which may last for several months and the use of a hose is prohibited.

If the water is strongly alkaline, it should not of course be used, and rain water is unlikely to be available in sufficient quantities for continual use outdoors. Do not use water softened artificially. Various modern overhead sprinklers are now on the market, mostly reliable, and many do not require much pressure.

Watering is best done in the early morning so as to soak in before the sun rises, and although no harm has been noticed by watering during strong sunlight at mid-day, there must be some evaporation.

Be cautious over using water with detergents in it. Bath water with soap is preferable.

5.3. Weedkillers and cultivation

It is only in the last few years that really suitable reliably safe weedkillers have come on the market. Before using herbicides all of the makers' instructions must be read very carefully. Avoid using a fine spray in windy weather so that drifting spray does not damage plants nearby. It is better to do the spraying oneself than entrust it to a jobbing gardener.

Rhododendrons and azaleas hate grass and other weeds growing on top of their shallow root system. With a knapsack sprayer or a watering can, it is easy to treat ground around established bushes.

Weedkillers can be divided into several groups. There are total weedkillers: sodium chlorate is the best known and is still the most effective, used at least six months before planting anything in the treated area. Simazine and relations are also total weedkillers of a kind, when used at high concentrations. Applied at lower concentrations, they are very good for killing germinating weed seeds in otherwise clean ground, but they are very persistent in the ground. They are also excellent on paths. 2,4,5,T is

17

very good against certain broadleaved herbaceous weeds, especially nettles. It is best applied in late spring. Most woody weeds grow again after the first application. Certain brands are rather volatile and give off fumes which can cause distortion in nearby young growth.

Paraquat is highly effective for burning off top growth of most weeds and is broken down in the soil immediately, except on peat and other pure organic matter. It is safe to use right up to the trunks of rhododendrons, but any drop which gets onto the foliage will cause a brown spot and it will damage green wood. It is relatively ineffective on nettles but severely checks bishops weed (*Aegopodium podagraria*); mosses are encouraged. It will be found necessary to apply it two or three times during the season for complete control of annual weeds.

As a general rule, rhododendrons should *not* be cultivated, because of their shallow root system. A careful shallow hoeing in dry weather does little harm, provided there are no roots on the surface. Deeper hoeing and digging or forking can damage the roots severely.

Rhododendrons appreciate loose, well aerated soil, as already stated. To keep carefully prepared beds and holes in good condition, avoid walking on them as much as possible. Regular paths should never cross within the area of roots, (root area is roughly similar to the branch spread) and beds should either be made narrow enough to reach from each side or have stepping stones strategically placed for walking on when weeding, and mulching.

5.4. Pruning and dead-heading
Pruning
Rhododendrons do not need regular pruning; only under special circumstances is any pruning necessary. Specimens retrieved from old collections are often lanky and drawn and in most cases respond well to cutting back. The chief exceptions are varieties with smooth bark, many of the big-leaved species, and the species of the Thomsonii and Taliense series. If pruning is necessary, it is generally better to cut back a portion at a time so that as many green leaves are left as possible. Certain varieties which grow away well, such as many hardy hybrids (especially those containing *R. ponticum* blood), the Triflorum and Lapponicum series, and deciduous azaleas, can break well from old wood. Even with them, it is safer not to be too drastic all at once.

Some dwarfs, notably in the Lapponicum series, can stand an occasional pruning with shears.

Cutting back is best done in the early spring or after flowering. Sometimes a little shaping can be done by cutting branches for indoor decoration. Always cut right back to a trunk or live shoot, dead stumps only encourage disease. It is seldom practical to reduce the overall dimension of a rhododendron by pruning. Usually the result is a ruined bush.

All rhododendrons look so much healthier if all dead wood is cut out. When doing this job, many half dead branches can also be removed.

Dead-heading. There is no doubt that the careful removal of dead rhododendron flowers, just after flowering, is beneficial to the plant and also promotes the formation of flower buds for the following year. Not only are dead seed heads often unsightly, but the production of seed in large quantities uses a considerable amount of energy.

It is simply not possible for most people to dead-head all their rhododendrons. Generally, those in most need of being done are the large-leaved species, which can form gigantic capsules. Certain dwarfs, such as *R. campylogynum* have long flower stalks and the seed capsules are set up well above the leaves. These can be removed quickly with a small pair of scissors. The removal of the larger flower heads can be speedily done by hand, once the knack is learned. Small trusses can be snapped off between finger and thumb. The largest varieties are better done with two hands as some force is needed and it is too easy to break off the whole shoot. Sometimes the trusses come away cleanly just above the topmost leaves, but in others it is just as well to knock off the individual spent flowers.

It is always worthwhile dead-heading newly planted specimens and of course any plants that appear to lack vigour or are not thriving.

6. Propagation

Even in the smallest garden, it is amusing to propagate something that is especially enjoyed by oneself.

Propagation can be divided into two completely separate sections. One is vegetative propagation, which means taking some part of an existing plant and making it into another plant, either by a cutting, layer or graft. Only in this way can something exactly similar to the original be produced. The other method is by seed. Even when the seed breeds true and is not deliberately or accidently hybridised, it will not give the exact replica of its parent. Therefore, hybrids and special clones should always be propagated vegetatively and only species and deliberate new crosses should be raised from seed.

6.1. Vegetative propagation
Cuttings. Great advances have been made in recent years in the art of rooting cuttings, and we now have the help of polythene, hormone rooting powders and automatic mist sprays. For the beginner wishing to grow just a handful of young plants, polythene is perhaps the greatest boon. Various propagation units are readily available such as trays with clear perspex lids, and some with electric heating. Even small mist units can be bought.

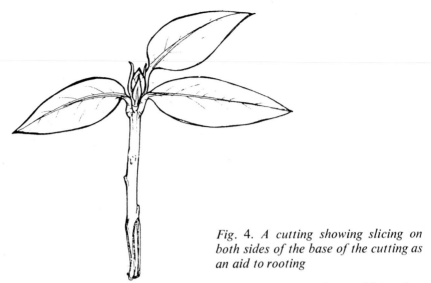

Fig. 4. A cutting showing slicing on both sides of the base of the cutting as an aid to rooting

These consist of an electric unit with overhead nozzles from which a fine spray is emitted; this is automatically controlled according to the sunlight. The greater the amount of sunshine the more frequent are the bursts of mist.

The two main points to remember when attempting to root any rhododendron cuttings are that the foliage must never be allowed to flag and that the drainage in the rooting medium must be perfect. Any more or less airtight container which does not receive the direct sun and yet lets in the maximum light, will prove suitable for the easier varieties. Outdoor frames at the back of a north wall are excellent and on a smaller scale, pots or boxes enclosed in a polythene bag and kept airtight can be successful. Any container used should be scrupulously clean. The best rooting medium is a 50/50 mixture of finest quality sphagnum peat and sharp sand or fine gravel. Whatever container is used, drainage should be put in the bottom in the form of clean broken crocks or large gravel. The rooting medium should be about 3 inches deep and must be renewed with each batch of cuttings.

The easiest cuttings to root and grow are Obtusum azaleas, and some dwarf rhododendrons such as *R. impeditum* and 'Elizabeth'. A few of the bigger hybrids are not too difficult.

Nearly all cuttings should be taken in a half ripe condition which means a cutting which will bend but will break if bent double. Most are ready in July and August, with a few not ripe enough until September. If taken too soft, the cuttings will rot and if too hard, they take much longer to root, if they root at all.

Cuttings of the dwarf alpine varieties and Obtusum azaleas should not be over 2 inches (5 cm) long and can be less. Larger varieties should be less than 4 inches (10 cm) long. Always use a sharp knife and cut cleanly through the wood. Only young growth should be used and there is no need to leave a heel of old wood, but if possible, cut at a node, trimming off the lower leaves. With some cultivars that are more difficult to root, slicing down each side of the base of the cutting may help to stimulate rooting. Most cuttings can be pushed into the rooting medium which should not be made too firm. Water in well.

Proprietary hormones can be used and are generally of some benefit. In a greenhouse, many cuttings will root in about three to four months. These can be put out into a cold frame after having been hardened off. Many cuttings are lost after they have rooted during the period of acclimatisation before planting out, and this must be done gradually. Another aid to rooting with more difficult cuttings is "bottom heat", when the rooting medium is heated at about 70°F. (21°C.) by thermostatically controlled electric cables laid at least 6 inches (15 cm) below the surface.

Potting soil. Any potting compost without chalk will suffice, but it should be loose and friable. If loam is used it must be of a light sandy nature. A good mixture is one half peat (preferably sphagnum and not too dusty) to a quarter oak or/and beech leaf-mould and a quarter coarse sand or fine gravel. Fertilizers may be added to speed up growth at the rate of 1 oz. superphosphate, $\frac{1}{2}$ oz. potassium sulphate, $\frac{1}{2}$ oz. ammonium sulphate and $\frac{1}{2}$ oz. magnesium sulphate (Epsom salts) per bushel.

When potting or boxing rooted cuttings, firm very lightly. A liquid foliar feed may be applied once a fortnight but stop this if any scorching of the leaves occurs.

Layering. This is perhaps the simplest method of propagation, and can be used for all varieties. Layering means placing a branch in soil while it is still attached to the parent plant and leaving it there until it is well rooted. This may take from one to three or even more years. Layering can be done where just one or more low branches are pegged down, or where a whole plant is layered, using every shoot possible. In the latter case, the root ball is often put on its side to ease the bending down of the branches. This method is commonly used in nurseries.

The simplest way to layer, is to select a low branch near the ground, dig out a little trench which should be filled with peat or a mixture of peat, sand and leaf-mould. Bend the branch at the tip into as upright a position as possible and hold it like this with a stake and some string. In an open or dry situation, do not mound up the soil over the branch. Only use relatively young shoots. Older ones will not bend easily, will take longer to root and will prove harder to establish, once removed from the parent.

In damp shady places, an excellent alternative to this method is to

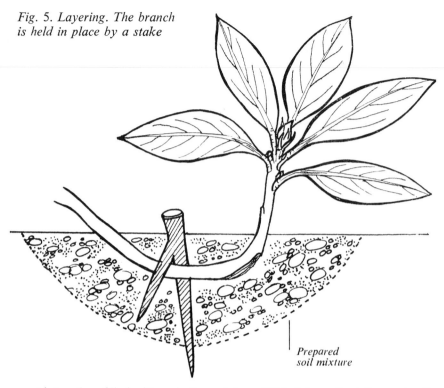

Fig. 5. Layering. The branch is held in place by a stake

*Prepared
soil mixture*

root into a box filled with a similar mixture. With this method the roots of the parent plant are not disturbed, it is often possible to use a branch at a higher level, and moving the layer after rooting is much easier. Flat stones may be placed on top of the branches, partly to hold them in position, and partly to retain moisture around the area of rooting. By bending of the shoot the rooted plant has a better shape and it also helps to speed up rooting. Slitting the stem at the bend can further stimulate the rooting.

When a good mat of roots has formed (which may take up to two years), the usual practice is to sever the branch just behind the roots but to leave the new plant in position for a few weeks or months before moving. It is best to establish new layers in a shady nursery bed before planting out into the final position.

Leggy specimens of dwarfs can be pegged down all round the perimeter and likewise bent into an upright posture by using stakes and string.

The great disadvantage of ground layering is that many specimens have no branches in reach of the soil. Air layering can be tried instead. This is done by wrapping sphagnum moss around a youngish shoot and

22

encasing this in polythene, securely taping each end.

One problem with this method is to stop water running down the stem and making the moss too wet for rooting. Air layering usually takes even longer than the first method and the severed layer is quite hard to establish.

Grafting. There are many different ways of grafting, but for rhododendrons, the simplest is a saddle graft. Grafting should be done only after all other methods of propagation have failed, i.e. layering is impossible, cuttings next to impossible to root and the particular qualities of the clone are unlikely to be repeated from seed.

Grafting can be done at various times of the year, but the best time is in mid-winter to March. Only vigorous young seedlings should be used as rootstocks, with a stem roughly equal to the thickness of the scion to be grafted. This should be about pencil thickness.

It is best to lift the stock about six weeks before the actual grafting is to take place, pot it up, and take it into heat to start the sap flowing. *Rhododendron ponticum* is the easiest stock to acquire and to work with, but its habit of producing suckers should rule out its use altogether. Almost any seedlings can be used, but *R. decorum* and *R. fortunei* are as good as any. For big-leaved species, any similar seedling stock will suffice.

When potting up the root stock, remove any side shoots or buds or leaves low down, so as to leave a clean stem for a few inches above soil

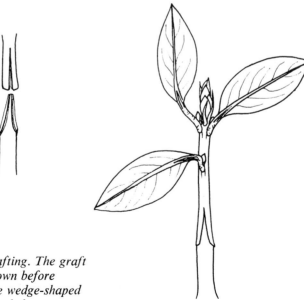

Fig. 6. Saddle grafting. The graft union, (left) is shown before binding: right, the wedge-shaped rootstock is shown below

23

level. Select only strong, healthy shoots for the scions. Cut a slice up each side of the stem of the root stock, with a sharp clean knife, for one to two inches (2.5 to 5 cm) to leave a wedge shape. Split the base of the scion to a similar distance up the stem; push the scion gently on to the wedge of severed stock and see that the bark coincides on one side at least. Bind tightly with a tape of polythene, a large rubber band cut open or raffia, dust with captan and place in an airtight frame or into a large polythene bag, with a couple of wire hoops to keep the bag off the foliage, and tie the top of the bag tightly. Shade from direct sunlight.

Callusing takes place quite rapidly in heat, but even after it is well callused, hardening off must be done extremely carefully. If the scion wilts, it invariably dies. Harden off over a period of several weeks, gradually allowing a little more air every few days. To overwinter, place in a shady position in the open or in a frame.

6.2. Propagation by seed

All rhododendron and azalea seed is small and light. It ripens from August to January but most capsules turn brown from October to December and must be watched carefully or much of the seed may be shed. Any seed collected at random in a collection of mixed varieties is liable to have been pollinated by bees, and so of mixed parentage. The only way to be sure that a species will come true to type is to hand pollinate. This is simply done

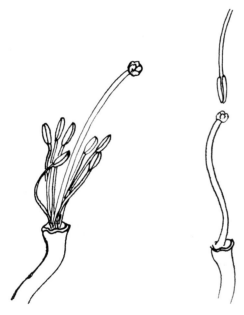

Fig. 7. *Preparing a flower for pollination: left, the corolla removed; right: the stamens removed leaving the pistil to be pollinated*

24

by first removing petals and stamens from a nearly open flower, being careful not to damage the pistil which is in the middle. Label carefully and two to three days later, apply pollen from the stamens, if possible off another plant of the same species, or if hybridising, from the intended male parent. Many rhododendrons are infertile with their own pollen.

After collection, the seed capsules should be dried carefully, either in an open container or in a packet, but not near direct heat. When the capsules split open, carefully shake out the seed and pick out bits of the capsule or other foreign matter as these encourage mould on the seed pan after sowing.

The seed can be stored in little envelopes in a closed tin for several months. With many varieties, the seed, if well stored will keep up to two years, but the Malesian species and hybrids must be sown as soon as the seeds are ripe.

One of the best sowing media is pure, finely sifted peat, which should be levelled out carefully and firmed in clean pans or boxes. Always soak the medium before sowing, from underneath, in soft water. Sow the seed thinly, especially the very small seed of dwarfs, and do not cover. Label, giving name, origin and the date sown. Sowing may be done in January if heat is available or postponed until March. Cover pans or boxes with clean glass and newspaper. The glass may be turned daily and no further watering should be necessary until well after germination, which begins two to three weeks later; then the glass is removed and a few days later the paper also. The young seedlings must never be allowed to dry out, and they must not stand in direct sunlight. Occasional watering should be done from below, by standing the pot or box in water and letting the water soak in gradually until the surface is moist. Syringing can also be done from above. Transplant into boxes or frames when big enough to handle. If the seeds have been sown thinly, this pricking out can be delayed until the following spring, but growth will be slower. Watch out for mould and apply the fungicide captan if necessary. Use the same compost for pricking out as for rooting cuttings.

A newer method of raising seedlings which takes less looking after at the early stages, is to use clear plastic food containers with air-tight lids. Fill the container to within an inch of the top, level out carefully and water and sow the seeds as before. When the first true leaves have appeared after the two cotyledons, gradually take off the lid for short periods during the day over a week or two. Thereafter treat as before.

7. Pests and Diseases

7.1. Pests

Although rhododendrons in general are relatively free from attacks by pests there are a few that can occasionally cause serious damage.

Caterpillars. In woodlands, various caterpillars eat the leaves of trees, such as oak, and these may attack the young leaves of rhododendrons growing beneath them. Spraying can be beneficial, but it is really easier to go round watching for the young caterpillars starting to eat, and kill them with the fingers and thumb.

Weevils. These cause similar damage to that of caterpillars, but only the edges of the leaves are usually attacked. These weevils usually eat at night and hide during the day. Dusting or spraying BHC on affected leaves and on the surrounding soil will destroy them. There is an alternative non-chemical method which can be equally effective. The weevils are local in their attack, do not travel far and also come out at night. By going out at night with a torch and a tray to bushes where the symptoms have been seen, it is possible to catch many of the weevils by holding the tray below the bush and giving it a sharp tap so that they drop on to the tray and can be removed.

Aphids can be troublesome in a greenhouse especially on the Malesian species and other young seedlings and Obtusum azaleas and also on the young growth of hardy hybrids outdoors. Control with malathion spray or aerosol.

Fig. 8. Weevil damage to rhododendron leaves

Mammals are much more damaging. Rabbits, roe and other deer hares and sheep are fond of many varieties, especially when young and newly planted. Those most liable to be attacked are all azaleas and many dwarf rhododendrons. If serious, wire netting is the only practical answer, other than destroying the culprits. Either the whole garden can be enclosed or individual susceptible specimens can be protected. Rabbits are only, likely to be really troublesome if plentiful. Dogs' (as opposed to bitches) urine, burns nasty holes in dwarf varieties and can even prove fatal. Moles loosen the soil and even throw young plants out of the soil. They are best trapped in their runs.

Birds. Tits ruin flowers particularly red ones, by pecking for nectar. Feeding with nuts and fat helps to keep the birds otherwise occupied!

Do keep human visitors from walking all over your beds!

7.2. Diseases

Likewise, diseases are usually of little consequence in Britain as only five are at all commonly met with. Possibly the most serious is honey fungus, *Armillaria mellea*. This normally lives on dead, woody tissue, but unfortunately it often attacks live plants as well. Those most susceptible are plants damaged by wind shake, waterlogging, or some other mechanical injury, usually at or below soil level. Some shrubs die off branch by branch, while others may suddenly collapse shortly after showing unhealthy foliage symptoms. Long brown or black boot-lace-like strands run through the soil, usually coming from rotting tree stumps and these start the infection.

Removal of all old stumps and dead rhododendrons helps to reduce its spread, but a possible new cure is refined creosote sold under the trade name of Armillatox. This can be used to sterilize infected soil and on tree stumps left in the ground. It is not, however, recommended for direct use on fibrous-rooted plants such as rhododendron.

Leaf spots. These black or brown spots on the leaves usually occur on badly drained or overshaded bushes, especially in a wet season. They are not serious except that they do show that the growing conditions could be improved. If the trouble persists, however, spray with a fungicide, such as captan or zineb, after flowering, repeating twice at 10- to 14-day intervals.

Petal blight. This is a comparatively new disease in Britain and attacks the flowers of Obtusum azaleas and other rhododendrons. It starts in damp weather as little brown spots on the flowers. These grow rapidly turning the whole flower into pulp which stick on the branches and remain very unsightly. Avoid overhead watering when the plants are in flower. If trouble is suspected, spray with zineb two or three times a week. Copper lime dust, spread all over the buds, is moderately effective.

Otherwise use bordeaux mixture or the new fungicide, benomyl. The latter need only be applied once a week.

Bud blast. This is not to be confused with frost damage. The flower buds die and little black spore-producing bristles cover the buds, which are not present when frosted. Only certain varieties are susceptible, notably *R. ponticum* and *R. caucasicum* and their hybrids. It is probably spread by the rhododendron leafhopper. Control of leafhoppers is difficult, but if bud blast is serious, some degree of control can be obtained by thorough and frequent spraying with malathion of the rhododendrons and surrounding area. Collect and burn affected buds.

Galls. These are common on Obtusum azaleas and the Ferrugineum series and its hybrids. They appear as ugly green, pink or red swellings on the leaves, stems or flowers and later turn white when sporing. It is worst in wet climates. Hand pick and burn, or spray with bordeaux mixture or zineb, as the new leaves appear.

Lichen. This is not a disease, rather a disfigurement. It is very common especially on azaleas in wet areas, more so on those which are lacking in vigour. Liberal top dressings (see p. 15) and cutting out old wood may

Fig. 9. Bud blast: a close-up of bristle-like fructifications of the fungus

help. If really bad, spray deciduous azaleas with lime sulphur (1 pint in 2 gallons of water) in the dormant season. No spray should be used on evergreen plants. Where there is only an odd bush with this trouble, scrub with carbolic soap and a nail brush.

7.3. Other Evils

Bark split. This injury is caused by early autumn or late spring frosts when the sap is running. Young growth is nearly always killed at the same time. The splitting of the bark can occur anywhere from ground level up to one-year-old shoots. The trouble is that it is not really noticeable until the bark is actually dead and curled back, by which time it is really too late to do much about it. If the stems, especially near ground level, are bound up with tape before this curling takes place, the bark may be saved. Protection of the base of the stem may be achieved either by wrapping it with old sacks or hessian or mounding up sawdust, pine needles, etc., temporarily, until the dangers of frost are over. This type of trouble usually takes place after a very early spring brings on young growth followed by a hard frost.

Secondary young growth usually comes away if the first flush is frosted, but it is never so robust and rarely sets flower buds. Partly frosted growth sometimes looks diseased with distorted, puckered, one-sided or even chlorotic leaves.

Chlorosis can develop for various reasons, such as inadequate drainage or exceptionally wet or dry seasons or from an imbalance of plant nutrients. It is very hard to recognise the various deficiencies or toxicities from the type of chlorosis present. If too much lime is not suspected, it is advisable to have the soil analysed and to get other professional advice.

Snow damage. Really heavy snowfalls, or late wet snow, can break branches of rhododendrons. Well grown, sturdy bushes with compact growth can usually withstand the weight, but open or leggy specimens may not be able to tolerate being bent right over. It is hard to know whether the snow should be shaken off or not.

Low growing and dwarf plants are well protected from frost by heavy snowfalls and therefore all snow should definitely be left on these.

8. Climate Problems

8.1. Hardiness

This is a subject that we are always learning more about. No two seasons are really alike and as a result, all plants including rhododendrons respond differently.

Damage from frost can be divided into two types: seasonable mid-winter frosts and unseasonable early autumn and late spring ones. The amount of damage caused by early and late spring frosts depends on the condition of the plants. In this country, there are very many rhododendron species and hybrids which can withstand almost any winter low temperature that we can produce, *provided* that they are dormant. It is the unseasonable frosts which cause so many failures (see barksplit and frosted young growth p. 29). Alternating warm and cold spells in winter result in the trusses of many rhododendrons opening with a few pips (buds) per truss destroyed.

A few people take no chances and grow only the toughest possible varieties, but many of these lack the interest and charm of the more tender ones. Surely it is worth taking a gamble! Given good growing conditions, many slightly vulnerable varieties will recover from any minor set-backs.

What can be done to alleviate frost damage? Shade and shelter are mentioned on p. 7. The use of fertilizers for hardening off is dealt with on p. 15. Well-grown bushes which have not been overfed with fertilizers are those most likely to withstand severe weather conditions. There is no doubt that overhead tree cover does give considerable protection in late spring and early autumn especially. Glass or plastic cloches are certainly beneficial to young or dwarf varieties and those of suspect hardiness should always be given some protection for the first years of their lives. Many species, particularly the large-leaved ones, such as *R. hodgsonii*, *R. macabeanum* and *R. calophytum* are very much more tender in their young immature state than after they reach 2 to 3 feet (61 to 91 cm.) and have developed their full-sized, mature leaves. Other means of protection are cold frames, rings of wire netting filled with bracken fronds, dry straw or leaves, or a hat of evergreen foliage. But beware of rotting the plants underneath!

8.2. What will grow where

From the point of view of rhododendron hardiness this country can be divided roughly into three zones of hardiness, as follows:

1. The west and south coastal districts, especially islands and peninsulas. These are the most favoured areas for growing tender varieties, such as the big-leaved species and the scented varieties. Much shelter is generally needed.

2. East and south-east coastal areas and low lying areas inland. Here much depends on the local situation. Bad frost pockets are only suitable for cast-iron or late-flowering varieties, but other more desirable sites will satisfy all but the most tender. Most of the Kurume azaleas are only good in southern districts.

3. All high ground above 500 feet approximately. Here the growing season is shorter with more early and late frosts and searing north winds, and one is restricted to dwarf and later flowering varieties. Obtusum azaleas are rarely satisfactory

9. Species and Hybrid Descriptions

There is now a vast array of both species and hybrids to choose from. In this booklet, a selection of the best is given. These include many of the old favourites and the best known modern varieties, plus a few which are still rare and only occasionally obtainable from nurseries, but which are of special merit. But the selection which follows is, to some extent, a personal one.

Nearly all species and many grex hybrids show great variability in growth and flower. In certain cases this amounts to excellent, good, bad and indifferent forms. In varieties that are easy to propagate regularly there is no excuse for the distribution of poor forms but occasionally this does still happen. Only the better forms (clones) should be bought, and with those species hard to propagate hand pollinated seedlings off good stock are often the best that can be obtained. Do not be tempted into buying bargain lots and if possible see the plants in flower at the nursery.

For simplification of choice, species and hybrids are grouped into four heights plus the big leaved and tender varieties.

To express the varying merits of the plants the following symbols are used for their characters, with further subdivisions by number:

H=Hardiness; four hardiness groups are designated from 1 to 4; the higher the number the hardier the plant.

H4 is hardy anywhere in Britain where rhododendrons will grow.

H3 suitable for the west, and for sheltered areas near south and east coast.

H2 for very sheltered gardens on the west coast.

H1 for greenhouse or sheltered walls.

F=Flower

L=Leaf

Qualifications given to plants for flower and leaf value are also numbered 1 to 4. The higher the number the better and 4 is excellent. In the lists below the months given are those of flowering.

The Royal Horticultural Society gives awards to plants which are considered to be especially noteworthy. These are given below (with date of award and flower colour) to help in selecting the better forms of the species The following awards are given to individual clones only and do not apply to every plant of a species or a hybrid grex group:

F.C.C. First Class Certificate. The highest award.

A.M. Award of Merit.

A.G.M. (The Award of Garden Merit) is given to a species as a whole and shows that it is a particularly good garden plant. The same applies to hybrids.

9.1. Species for Outdoors

(a) LARGE LEAVED. All these eventually reach 20 ft. (6.1 m.) or more and take some years to reach flowering size. Plenty of shelter is necessary with partial shade.

R. calophytum H4 F2-4 (Mar. Apr.) L2-4

A fine early flowering species, with leaves up to 15 in. (38 cm.) long. Large many flowered trusses of bell-shaped flowers, white to pink with a deep blotch. A.M. 1920 to form with white flushed pink flowers; F.C.C. 1933 to form with pale pink flowers.

R. falconeri H3-4 F3-4 (Apr. May) L3-4

Extremely handsome when well grown under woodland conditions. Fine leaves, rough above, and covered with dense rust-coloured indumentum below. Big trusses of long lasting creamy-white to pale yellow flowers with a purple blotch, 2½ in. (6.3 cm.) long. It grows best in the west, but is satisfactory in most other sheltered areas. A.M. 1922.

R. fictolacteum H4 F2-4 (Apr. May) L2-3

The best of this type for colder gardens. Excellent dark green foliage with buff to rusty indumentum below, most attractive with the sun on it. Compact trusses of white to rose tinted flowers with a dark crimson blotch, 2 in. (5 cm.) long. A.G.M. 1968; A.M. 1923 white with crimson blotch; A.M. 1953 'Cherry Tip' white flushed pink with deep crimson blotch. The similar *R. rex* has larger leaves and flowers.

R. hodgsonii H4 F2-3 (Apr.) L2-3

A grand foliage plant. The large leaves have a metallic sheen above, and grey to fawn indumentum below. Large trusses of upstanding flowers, rose pink to dark magenta-purple. Most attractive smooth peeling reddish brown bark. Quite hardy in a sheltered situation but tender when very young. A.M. 1964 'Poet's Lawn' flowers shaded reddish-purple.

R. macabeanum H3-4 F3-4 (Mar. Apr.) L3-4

One of the finest yellow flowered species in cultivation and a spectacular foliage plant. Leaves up to 12 in. (30.5 cm.) long, dark shiny green above and white indumentum below. Flowers in huge trusses, creamy yellow to deep yellow in the best forms, fleshy, bell-shaped, with a purple blotch; up to 3 in. (7.6 cm.) long. Hardy in most favoured gardens throughout Britain. F.C.C. 1938 to a yellow flowered form.

R. sinogrande H3-4 F3-4 (Apr.) L4

Has the largest leaves of all rhododendrons, up to 2½ ft. (0.76 m.) or more long when young; glossy above and silvery grey to fawn skin-like indumentum below. Flowers in enormous trusses, waxy, bell-shaped and long lasting, dull creamy white to pale yellow. Rarely grows well away from the very sheltered west coast gardens. Tender when young. F.C.C. 1926 ivory white with crimson blotch; A.M. 1922 creamy-white with crimson blotch.

32

(b) TALL. 15 ft. (4.6 m.) or more. To grow well, these require shelter and some shade.

R. arboreum H2-4 F3-4 (Jan. Apr.) L3-4

One of the few rhododendrons that often develops a single trunk and can reach 40 ft. (12.2 m.) or more in favoured localities. A very variable species. Rigid leaves up to 8 in. (20.2 cm.) long, white, fawn, cinnamon to rusty brown below. Flowers in dense rounded trusses, blood-red, pink to white, sometimes spotted. The blood-red forms are the most tender, and can only be grown in really mild areas. Very showy in full flower. A.M. 1964 'Goat Fell', cherry colour.

R. barbatum H3-4 F3-4 (Mar.) L2-3

Develops into a nicely shaped large bush if given space. Leaves up to 8 in. (20.3 cm.) long; leaf stalks and branchlets usually clad with long bristles. Flowers in round compact trusses, of a fine scarlet. Rather early flowering. Hardy in most areas of Britain. A.M. 1954.

R. decorum H3-4 F2-3 (May June) L2-3

In the hardier forms, this is the most generally suitable of the larger species for growing all over the country. Leaves up to 6 in. (15 cm.) long. Flowers in a flat-topped truss, white to shell pink with or without spots, scented. Very easily grown and is one of the most lime tolerant species.

R. fargesii (including *R. oreodoxa*) H4 F2-4 (Mar. Apr.) L2-3

One of the most free flowering of the larger species. Neat leaves up to 3½ in. (8.9 cm.) long. Flowers in loose trusses, bell-shaped, rose to white, with or without spots. Very hardy and easily grown. Quite tolerant of lime. A.M. 1926, rose pink, dotted dark crimson.

R. rubiginosum H4 F2-3 (Mar. May) L1-2

This attractive, free flowering, comparatively small-leaved species stands up well to wind and is good for interior windbreaks. Dark green leaves up to 2½ in. (6.3 cm.) long, rust coloured below. Flowers funnel-shaped, rosy lilac, pink to almost white, spotted brown. Grows quite well on lime. A.M. 1960 'Wakehurst' mallow-purple with crimson spots. The closely related *R. desquamatum* has longer narrower leaves and larger flatter flowers but is more tender.

R. sutchuenense H4 F2-4 (Feb. Mar.) L2-3

A very fine species with quite large leaves up to 12 in. (30 cm.) long. Flowers in large, many-flowered trusses, rosy lilac, rosy pink or white stained pink. Rather early flowering but hardy. Needs plenty of room to grow. A.M. 1945 with a deep purplish blotch.

R. thomsonii H4 F3-4 (Mar. May) L2-3

Magnificent when covered with deep blood-red waxy flowers. The leaves in many forms have a glaucous bloom above and the bark is smooth and peeling. Leaves up to 3½ in. (8.9 cm.) long. Flowers in loose trusses. A.G.M. 1968.

(c) MEDIUM. 8-15 ft. (2,4-4.6 m.). Best grown under woodland conditions or where there is some shade and shelter. This group includes nearly all the Triflorum series which have rather thin branches, small scaly leaves, and plentifully produced butterfly-like flowers in small trusses.

R. augustinii H3-4 F2-4 (Apr. May) L1-2

The nearest to blue of the larger species. A Triflorum. Very effective in masses. Leaves up to 5 in. (12.7 cm.) long. Flowers usually pale lavender-blue to intense violet. The deepest blue forms are the most tender. The others will grow in most parts of Britain, but all are liable to barksplit after unseasonable frosts. Quite lime tolerant. A.M. 1926; A.G.M. 1968.

R. campanulatum H3-4 F1-4 (Apr. May) L2-4

A very variable species with many different forms in cultivation. Leaves up to 6 in. (15 cm.) long, dark glossy green above, and clad underneath with thick to thin fawn to rusty brown indumentum. The flowers are in compact or loose trusses in many shades of purple, mauve, rosy white or white, usually well spotted. Often a fine foliage plant. Most introductions are hardy but some suffer from barksplit. A.M. 1964 'Roland Cooper' white shaded mauve; A.M. 1965 'Waxen Bell' phlox purple, spotted pansy purple.

R. campylocarpum H3-4 F3-4 (Apr.) L2

One of the finest yellow flowered species. Leaves up to 4 in. (10 cm.) long, dark glossy green above. Flowers in loose trusses, bell-shaped, canary yellow to pale yellow. Suitable for all but the very coldest gardens in Britain. F.C.C. 1892.

R. cinnabarinum H3-4 F3-4 (Apr. July) L2-3

A most unusual and beautiful species with waxy tubular, mostly pendent flowers. Many forms occur with different leaves, flowers and times of flowering. Leaves up to 3 in. (7.6 cm.) long, glaucous to dark green above. Flowers in small loose trusses, cinnabar red, crimson, pale pinkish purple, plum purple, or orange or with a combination of red, yellow and apricot. Most forms are fairly hardy, but some are subject to barksplit and subsequent die-back. A.M. 1945 to var. *blandfordiaeflorum;* A.M. 1953 'Vin Rosé' a clone of var. *roylei;* A.M. 1951 var. *purpurellum.*

R. concinnum var. *pseudoyanthinum* H4 F2-3 (Apr. May) L1-2

Triflorum series. The flowers are an unusual, striking colour. Leaves up to 3½ in. (8.9 cm.) long, dark green above. Flowers deep rosy purple to ruby red, up to 1½ in. (3.8 cm.) long. Hardy. A.M. 1951.

R. davidsonianum H3-4 F2-4 (Apr. May) L1-2

Another Triflorum. The best forms are a most lovely delicate pink. Leaves up to 3 in. (7.6 cm.) long. Flowers pink to white tinged pink or pale purplish rose. Fairly lime resistant. A.G.M. 1968. F.C.C. 1955 pale rose form; Preliminary award (American) 'Ruth Lyons' clear pink.

R. irroratum H3-4 F2-4 (Mar. May) L2-3

In this variable species, the white forms are the most charming. Leaves up to 5 in. (12.7 cm.) long. Flowers in loose or fairly compact trusses, white, creamy yellow to dull rose, with or without many crimson or greenish spots. A.M. 1957 white tinged bluish pink; A.M. 1957 'Polka Dot' white, heavily spotted purple.

R. lutescens H3-4 F1-4 (Feb. Apr.) L2-3

A most dainty early flowering yellow species in the Triflorum series, with interesting bronzy-red new growth. Leaves narrow, up to $3\frac{1}{2}$ in. (8.9 cm.) long. Flowers pale to deeper primrose-yellow, spotted light green, The award forms have fine large flowers. Not too hardy in cold areas. A.G.M. 1968. F.C.C. 1938 clear lemon-yellow; A.M. 1953 'Bagshot Sands' primrose yellow flowers.

R. oreotrephes H4 F2-3 (Apr. May) L1-3

A beautiful plant (Triflorum series), in the best forms with fine glaucous young foliage and lovely rose pink flowers. Leaves up to $4\frac{1}{2}$ in. (11.4 cm.) long, usually much less, sometimes semi-deciduous. Flowers mauve, mauve-pink, purple or rose, rarely white. Best grown in an open fairly sunny position to keep it compact. A.M. 1932 rosy purple; A.M. 1935 bright pinkish mauve with darker spots; A.M. 1937 light pinkish mauve, red spotted.

R. souliei H4 F2-4 (May) L2-3

One of the most beautiful of all species and should be in every garden. Almost round leaves up to 3 in. (7.6 cm.) long. Lovely saucer-shaped flowers, soft or deeper rose or white, 2 in. (5 cm.) or more across. Does well in dry areas. F.C.C. 1909 pale rose, deeper towards edge; F.C.C. 1936 with deeper pink flowers than above; F.C.C. 1951 Windsor Park form, white with deep pink flush at margins and small crimson blotch.

R. wardii H4 F2-4 (May June) L2-3

A first-class yellow-flowered species, very variable. Leaves up to 4 in. (10 cm.) long. Flowers in loose trusses, saucer-shaped, bright or clear lemon-yellow, sometimes with a crimson blotch. Some of the Ludlow and Sheriff introductions are especially good. A.G.M. 1968. A.M. 1926 bright yellow with a touch of crimson; A.M. 1931 bright yellow flushed green; A.M. 1959 'Ellesstee' (Ludlow, Sherriff and Taylor) with a deep crimson blotch; A.M. 1963 'Meadow Pond' (Ludlow and Sherriff.)

R. yunnanense H3-4 F2-4 (May) L1-2

An exceedingly valuable species of the Triflorum series, which should be in every garden. Leaves up to 4 in. (10 cm.) long. Flowers pink, white, pale rose-lavender or lavender. Always smothers itself in flower from an early age and is easily grown. Quite hardy but is occasionally liable to barksplit from a late frost. A.G.M. 1968. A.M. 1903.

(d) LOW. 4-8 ft. (1.22-2.44 m.). For near the front of borders or light woodland.

R. aberconwayi H4 F2-4 (May June) L1-2

In the best forms, this is a beautiful species. Leaves up to 4 in. (10 cm.) long, with a hard and thick texture. Flowers white or white tinged pink, more or less spotted with crimson, flat in upstanding trusses. A.M. 1945 'His Lordship.'

R. bureavii H4 F2-3 (Apr. May) L3-4

One of the finest foliage plants in the genus. Leaves up to 5 in. (12.7 cm.) long, thick and leathery; the underside and branchlets are covered with thick rusty red woolly indumentum. Flowers in compact trusses, white or rose with crimson markings, up to 2 in. (5 cm.) long. Slow to flower. Unfortunately not always available from nurseries. A.M. 1939.

R. callimorphum H3-4 F3-4 (May June) L2-3

A first-rate species for the small garden. Leaves up to 3 in. (7.6 cm.) long, almost round. Flowers soft to deep rose in a loose truss. The lovely flowers, freely produced, are set off well by the attractive foliage. Worth trying in any sheltered position but liable to barksplit.

R. ciliatum H3-4 F2-3 (Mar. Apr.) L1-2

An attractive early, free-flowering species, unfortunately very easily frosted. Leaves up to $3\frac{1}{2}$ in. (8.9 cm.) long, hairy. Flowers white or pink tinged, narrowly bell-shaped, up to 2 in. (5 cm.) across. Good for edging a border. Not suitable for the coldest gardens. A.M. 1953 white, slightly tinged pink.

R. concatenans H3-4 F2-3 (Apr. May) L2-4

A really striking plant with lovely glaucous foliage and apricot to yellow waxy flowers. Leaves up to $2\frac{1}{2}$ in. (6.3 cm.) long. Flowers in loose trusses. Quite compact if not grown in too much shade. F.C.C. 1935.

R. dauricum H4 F2-3 (Jan. Mar.) L1-2

The earliest species to flower. Leaves up to $1\frac{1}{2}$ in. (3.8 cm.) long, semi-evergreen or deciduous. Flowers bright rose purple to bright purple or rarely white, surprisingly frost hardy. They are very freely produced and it is a real harbinger of spring. The closely related *R. mucronulatum* has longer leaves. A.G.M. 1968; F.C.C. 1969 'Midwinter' semi-deciduous.

R. degronianum H4 F1-3 (Apr. May) L2-3

A neat plant, often compact. Leaves up to 6 in. (15 cm.) long, with fawn to rufous indumentum below. Flowers in loose trusses, clear soft pink with deeper lines, up to $2\frac{1}{2}$ in. (6.3 cm.) across. Desirable in the better forms.

R. dichroanthum H3-4 F1-3 (May June) L1-2

A very variable species, well worth growing the best orange introductions. Leaves up to 4 in. (10 cm.) long, with white, grey or fawn indumentum below. Flowers deep or dull orange to salmon-pink or yellowish copper. A.M. 1923, orange-red.

R. didymum H4 F2-3 (June July) L1-2

Most useful is its late flowering season. Leaves up to 2½ in. (6.3 cm.) long, dark green above, with grey-white indumentum below. Flowers black-crimson, waxy, in loose trusses, up to 2 in. (5 cm.) long. Best seen with the sun behind the flowers. Fairly hardy.

R. glaucophyllum H4 F2-3 (Apr. May) L1-2

A very free flowering species with aromatic foliage. Leaves up to 3½ in. (8.9 cm.) long, glaucous white underneath. Flowers bell-shaped in a loose truss, pink, rose or pinkish-purple, rarely white. Excellent for the edge of woodland. var. *tubiforme* flowers more tubular. var. *luteiflorum* (H3 Mar. Apr.) beautiful lemon-yellow flowers. The last form a little tender. F.C.C. 1966 'Glen Cloy'.

R. griersonianum H3-4 F3-4 (June) L2-3

Has beautiful geranium-scarlet flowers, freely produced. Very distinct and desirable. Soft leaves, rather narrow, up to 8 in. (20.3 cm.) long, with white to buff woolly indumentum below. Flowers funnel-shaped in loose trusses. Tender when young. Worth trying in most sheltered districts. F.C.C. 1924.

R. haematodes H4 F3-4 (May June) L2-3

A first-class species with neat attractive foliage. Leaves up to 3 in. (7.5 cm.) long, dark green above. Both young shoots and leaf undersides are covered with dense woolly indumentum. Flowers fleshy, brilliant scarlet-crimson to scarlet, in loose trusses, up to 2 in. (5 cm.) long. A little slow to flower but well worth waiting for. Quite hardy. F.C.C. 1926.

R. neriiflorum H3-4 F3-4 (Apr. May) L1-2

One of the best red, scarlet or crimson species. Leaves up to 4 in. (10 cm.) long. Flowers waxy, in loose trusses, up to 2 in. (5 cm.) long. Many forms are unfortunately only suited to mild areas but selected introductions are reasonably hardy. Very variable.

R. orbiculare H4 F2-3 (Mar. Apr.) L2-3

A lovely foliage plant when well grown. Leaves up to 4 in. (10 cm.) long, almost round, bright green. Flowers rose-pink to rose in loose trusses. To develop a perfect dome-shaped specimen, do not plant in too much shade and allow plenty of room. A.M. 1922.

R. pseudochrysanthum H4 F3-4 (Apr.) L2-3

A fine species still little known. Leaves densely crowded, up to 3 in. (7.5 cm.) long, thick and leathery with indumentum on the midrib below. Flowers pale pink to white with rose lines and crimson spots, up to 2 in. (5 cm.) long. Usually compact, with nice, unusual foliage and most attractive flowers. A.M. 1956 white flushed pink with crimson spots.

R. racemosum H4 F1-3 (Mar. Apr.) L1-2

A most adaptable species, occurring in many forms from a dwarf up to 10 ft. (3.05 m.). Leaves up to 2 in. (5 cm.) long, very glaucous below.

Flowers axillary, often all up the top 3-4 in. (7.5-10 cm.) of the shoots; pink, pale to deep rose or white, up to nearly 1 in. (2.5 cm.) long. The best dwarf forms grow under the collector's number Forrest 19404. A.G.M. 1968; A.M. 1970 'Rock Rose'; F.C.C. 1892.

R. wasonii H4 F2-3 (Apr. May) L2-3

A handsome foliaged species of good habit when well grown and with fine yellow flowers. Leaves up to 4 in. (10 cm.) long, with indumentum below, at first white, later rusty red. Flowers in loose trusses, creamy white to pale yellow; crimson spots. Var. *rhododactylum* has pinkish flowers.

(e) DWARFS. 4 ft. (1.22 m.) and under. For rockgardens and peat borders in at least half sunshine, especially in the north.

R. calostrotum H4 F2-4 (May) L1-3

One of the most beautiful of all the dwarfs. Leaves usually glaucous green above, up to 1⅓ in. (3.5 cm.) long. Flowers bright rose-crimson to rich purple. Almost flat, and large for the size of the plant; very freely produced. A.G.M. 1968 (red form); F.C.C. 1971 'Gigha' bright rose-crimson; A.M. 1935 deep rosy-mauve to magenta: var. *calciphilum* smaller leaves and pink flowers.

R. campylogynum H3-4 F2-3 (May June) L2-3

A very variable species with the neatest little thimble-like flowers on long flower stalks. Leaves up to 1 in. (2.5 cm.) long, usually glaucous below. Flowers claret, salmon-pink to pale rose-purple or black-purple, or cream coloured. Gems for the rockgarden. Nearly all are hardy. A.M. 1966 'Thimble' salmon-pink flowers: var. *myrtilloides* very dwarf with small flowers: var. *charopoeum* the largest flowered variety: var. *celsum* the tallest, with erect habit: var. *cremastum* leaves green underneath.

R. camtschaticum H4 F2-3 (May) L2-3

A most unusual deciduous species which flowers on the young wood. Leaves up to 2 in. (5 cm.) long, hairy. Flowers reddish purple, spotted, nearly flat, about 1½ in. (3.8 cm.) across. Easily grown in Scotland but more difficult in the south of England. Grow in full sun in the north.

R. cephalanthum H4 F2-3 (Apr. May) L1-2

Delightful small trusses of daphne-like tubular flowers. Leaves up to 1½ in. (3.8 cm.) long, aromatic. Flowers white or pink, up to ¾ in. (1.9 cm.) long. Excellent for rockgardens or peat walls. Var. *crebreflorum* is one of the loveliest of all dwarfs. Very low, with pink flowers.

R. chamae-thomsonii H4 F2-3 (Mar. Apr.) L1-2

The larger growing equivalent of *R. forrestii* var. *repens*. Leaves up to 3½ in. (8.8 cm.) long, usually much less. Flowers crimson or scarlet to pink, rather tubular, waxy. Very variable, some forms flower quite freely. Hardy but early flowering. Var. *chamaethauma* is a dwarfer smaller leaved form. A.M. 1932.

R. chryseum H4 F2-3 (Apr. May) L1-2

One of the few yellow Lapponicums, which looks excellent grown alongside the other predominantly mauve to blue species. Leaves up to ½ in. (1.3 cm.) long. Flowers pale to bright yellow. Hardy in most forms.

R. ferrugineum H4 F1-2 (June) L1-2

The well known dwarf from the Alps of Europe. Leaves up to 1½ in. (3.8 cm.) long. Flowers tubular, rosy-crimson or white. Very hardy. A.M. 1969 *ferrugineum album* white flowers. The similar *R. hirsutum* will grow on moderately alkaline soils.

R. forrestii H4 F1-4 (Mar. May) L1-2

When well flowered, this is quite one of the finest dwarfs, but many forms rarely flower. Leaves up to 1½ in. (3.8 cm.) long, purple underneath. Flowers bright scarlet, tubular, waxy. Var. *repens* is the more usual variety. Leaves green underneath, prostrate habit. F.C.C. 1935. Var. *tumescens* dome shaped habit. All are hardy except for the young growth, some shade is needed.

R. hanceanum H4 F2-3 (May) L1-2

A distinct species with rather narrow cream to yellow flowers, many per truss. Leaves up to 5 in. (12.7 cm.) long, usually much less, thick and leathery. Flowers up to 1 in. (2.5 cm.) long. A.M. 1957 'Canton Consul', cream coloured. 'Nanum' (F3) is very dwarf and compact with bright yellow flowers freely produced. A first rate dwarf, hardy.

R. hippophaeoides H4 F2-3 (Mar. May) L2-3

A handsome easily grown rather upright semi-dwarf, growing up to 5 ft. (1.52 m.). Leaves up to 1¼ in. (3.1 cm.) long, slightly glaucous green. Flowers usually lavender-blue. A.G.M. 1968; A.M. 1927 lavender-blue.

R. impeditum H4 F3-4 (Apr. May) L2-3

One of the best dwarfs for general garden use. Leaves about ½ in (1.3 cm.) long. Flowers mauve or light purplish blue, about ⅔ in. (1.6 cm.) long. Similar to *R. fastigiatum* but even more compact with less glaucous leaves. Very hardy and free flowering. A.G.M. 1968; A.M. 1944.

R. lepidostylum H4 F1 (May June) L3-4

The finest glaucous foliage plant among the dwarfs. Leaves especially blue when young, about 1½ in. (3.8 cm.) long. Flowers yellow, often hidden in the foliage. Should be in every garden. A.M. 1969 for foliage.

R. leucaspis H3-4 F3-4 (Mar. Apr.) L2-3

A really beautiful plant when it escapes the frost. Leaves up to 2½ in. (6.3 cm.) long, with hairy margins. Flowers flat, milky white with chocolate brown stamens. Not for really cold gardens. Very good in a pot. F.C.C. 1944; A.M. 1929 to form with a touch of sulphur within the flowers.

R. microleucum H4 F3 (Apr.) L2

Pretty little pure white flowers which contrast well with the earlier mauve and blue varieties. Leaves up to ⅔ in. (1.6 cm.) long. Surprisingly frost resistant flowers. F.C.C. 1939.

R. moupinense H4 F3-4 (Feb. Mar.) L1-2

A lovely harbinger of spring, well worth the risk of frost. Leaves up to 1½ in. (3.8 cm.) long, shiny above, thick and leathery. Flowers white, pink or deep rose. Best planted under trees away from the early morning sun. Hardy but likes perfect drainage. A.M. 1914 white flowers 2 in. (5 cm.) across; A.M. 1937 flowers heavily suffused with rose-pink.

R. pemakoense H4 F2-3 (Mar. Apr.) L1-2

Masses of comparatively large flowers can completely hide the foliage in favourable seasons. Leaves up to 1¼ in. (3.2 cm.) long. Flowers pale pinkish purple to pale purple, up to 1½ in. (3.8 cm.) long. Easily grown, but the flower buds are often frosted. Sometimes stoloniferous. Hardy as a plant. A.G.M. 1968; A.M. 1933, white flowers suffused with mauve.

R. radicans H4 F2-3 (May June) L1-2

A creeping mat-like shrub with the flowers held well above the foliage. Leaves up to ¾ in. (1.9 cm.) long, shiny above. Flowers almost flat, pale to dark purple, ¾ in. (1.9 cm.) long. An excellent ground cover for peat walls and useful for the lateness of the flowers. A.M. 1926, rosy purple flowers, 1 in (2.5 cm.) across. *R. keleticum* is slightly larger in all parts.

R. russatum H4 F3-4 (Apr. May) L1-2

The finest species of this colour in the genus with bright deep reddish to blue-purple flowers. Leaves about 1 in. (2.5 cm.) long. A.G.M. 1968; F.C.C. 1933, intense purple; A.M. 1927, violet-blue.

R. sargentianum H4 F2-3 (Apr. May) L1-2

One of the neatest dwarfs with charming little cream to yellow flowers. Leaves up to ¾ in. (1.9 cm.) long. Flowers about ½ in. (1.3 cm.) across. Very compact habit. Hardy, and slow growing. Appreciates a little shade. A.M. 1923, pale yellow; A.M. 1966, 'Whitebait', cream.

R. scintillans H4 F2-4 (Apr. May) L1-2

In the best forms, this is the nearest to a true blue of all rhododendrons. Leaves up to ½ in. (1.3 cm.) long. Flowers very freely produced, lavender to almost a royal-blue, about ½ in. (1.3 cm.) long. A.G.M. 1968; F.C.C. 1934, lavender-blue; A.M. 1924, purplish rose.

R. trichostomum H3-4 F2-3 (May June) L1-2

Round trusses of pink, rose or white flowers, most showy, long lasting and attractive in the best selections. Leaves up to 1⅓ in. (3.3 cm.) long. Flowers like a daphne, about ¾ in. (1.9 cm.) long. A few forms are rather tender. A.M. 1960, rose suffused white.

R. williamsianum H.4 F2-3 (Apr.) L2-3

A beautiful dome-shaped shrub with lovely bell-shaped flowers, showing up well against the nearly round leaves. Leaves up to 1¾ in. (4.4 cm.) long. Hardy as a plant but the pretty young growth gets frosted in some areas. A.M. 1938.

R. yakusimanum H4 F3-4 (May) L2-3

Perhaps the most sought-after of all rhododendron species. Pale pink flowers, fading to white, in compact truss over fine dark foliage on perfect dome-shaped bush. Leaves about $3\frac{1}{2}$ in. (8.9 cm.) long, recurved, with thick, light buff indumentum below. A.G.M. 1968. F.C.C 1947

9.2. Tender Species For indoors or very mild sheltered gardens.

R. ciliicalyx H1-2 F3-4 (Mar. Apr.) L1-2

A beautiful scented species for a cool greenhouse. Height to 10 ft. (3.05 m.). Leaves up to $3\frac{1}{2}$ in. (8.9 cm.) long. Flowers white or suffused with pale rose, 4 in. (10 cm.) across. A.M.1923.

R. crassum H2-3 F2-3 (June July) L2-3

One of the hardiest of the strongly scented species. Height to 15 ft. (4.57 m.) often less. Leaves up to 5 in. (12.7 cm.) long, dark green, glossy and thick. Flowers white, or white tinged pink. Reasonably hardy in very sheltered gardens. A.M. 1924, white flowers.

R. edgeworthii H2-3 F2-4 (Apr. May) L3-4

One of the best scented species. Lovely flowers and fine foliage. Height occasionally to 10 ft. (3.05 m.), often straggly. Leaves about 4 in. (10 cm.) long, dark green and rough above; cobwebby indumentum below. Flowers 4 in. (10 cm.) across, white or tinged pink, deliciously fragrant. Some forms are hardy in a well sheltered garden if given perfect drainage. F.C.C. 1933.

R. lindleyi H1-3 F4 (Apr. May) L2-3

Beautiful large scented flowers. A wonderful plant. Height to 15 ft (4.57 m.), unfortunately of rather a leggy habit. Leaves up to 6 in. (15.2 cm.) long. Flowers white or cream with a yellow blotch, sometimes flushed with rose, almost lily-shaped, about 5 in. (12.7 cm.) across. The Ludlow and Sherriff introduction is the hardiest, but most will survive in warm, west-coast gardens. F.C.C. 1937, white with pink tips; A.M. 1935 white flushed with rose; A.M. 1969, 'Geordie Sherriff', white strongly flushed rose.

MALESIAN RHODODENDRONS

This group comes from the tropical regions between Malaya and North Queensland, Australia. They are not used to winter and summer seasons and therefore cannot tolerate our cold winters. Many species occur and most of these can be grown successfully in pots or very carefully drained beds in a frost-free greenhouse. Flower size varies from small narrow tubes to large and showy. Nearly all tend to be rather straggly in habit and vary in height from a few inches to many feet. Several are scented.

Over half a century ago these were popular indoor plants and many hybrids were raised, known as 'Javanese hybrids'. Their popularity died out and so did many of the cultivars grown. Now, with much of the mainland Asia being closed to plant collectors, attention is being drawn towards Borneo and New Guinea especially and many hitherto unknown species are being introduced. Very few are at present available from nurseries, but as interest in these plants increases, the finest species and hybrids may become obtainable. Many are very beautiful and are well worth a place in a cool house.

Amongst the best species are *R. aurigeranum*, orange-yellow; *R. christi*, red; *R. christianae*, deep yellow, shaded orange; *R. gracilentum*, pink or red, dwarf; *R. javanicum*, yellow to scarlet; *R. konori*, white; *R. laetum*, deep yellow; *R. lochae*, scarlet; and *R. zoelleri*, yellow to salmon.

9.3. Hybrids

In the tables which follow stars are also given to the rhododendrons. These indicate general merit, with four stars meaning excellent, and one star, of fair value. Plants of recent introduction are marked 'new'.

The names indented are those of clones that belong to the grex, and the figures for hardiness and flower value, and months of flowering are the same as for the grex: the clones may differ in merit and flower colour.

A. TALL. 15 feet or more: 4.57 m. or more
for a woodland site, fairly sheltered

Name	H	F	Flower colour	Time	Award	
Albatross ****	4	4	white, large	June	A.M.	1934
					A.G.M.	1968
Exbury Albatross			blush-pink		F.C.C.	1955
Angelo****	3	3–4	blush-pink	June		
Exbury Angelo			white		F.C.C.	1947
Avalanche	3	4		Mar. Apr.		
Alpine Glow ***			white		A.M.	1935
unnamed form ***			pink		F.C.C.	1938
Loderi	3–4	3–4				
King George ****			pink, fading to white		A.M.	1968
					A.G.M.	1968
Pink Diamond ****			pink		A.G.M.	1968
Venus ****			pale pink		A.G.M.	1968
Julie ***			cream			
Penjerrick ****	3	4	white, creamy-yellow, or pink	May	A.M.	1923
Polar Bear ***	3–4	4	white, scented	July Aug.	F.C.C.	1946

B. MEDIUM. 8–15 feet: 2.44–4.57 m.
for woodland conditions, the middle of borders or as specimen plants

Name	H	F	Flower colour	Time	Award	
A. Bedford ***	4	3	lavender	June	A.M.	1936
					F.C.C.	1958
Azor ****	3–4	4	salmon	July Aug.	A.M.	1933
Beauty of Littleworth ****	4	4	white	May	F.C.C.	1953
Betty Wormald ****	4	4	pink	May June	F.C.C.	1968
Carita	4	3–4	yellow to biscuit rose	May		
A. M. clone **			yellow		A.M.	1945
Inchmery **			biscuit tinged rose			
Golden Dream ***			golden yellow			
Crest ****	4	4	yellow	May	F.C.C.	1953
Cynthia ***	4	4	rose-crimson	May June	A.G.M.	1968

42

Name	H	F	Flower colour	Time	Award	
David **	4	3	blood red	May	F.C.C.	1939
					A.M.	1957
Earl of Donoughmore ***	4	4	bright red	May June		
Fastuosum Flore Pleno ****	4	4	mauve	June	A.G.M.	1928
Furnival's Daughter ****	4	4	pink, heavily spotted	May June	F.C.C.	1961
Idealist ***	4	4	greenish yellow	May	A.M.	1948
Lady Bessborough F.C.C. ****	4	4	pale yellow	May		
Roberte ***	4	4	pink		F.C.C.	1936
Lady Chamberlain F.C.C. ****	3–4	3–4	orange-salmon	May	F.C.C.	
Lady Rosebery ****	3–4	4	pink	May		
Lavender Girl ****	4	4	lavender	May June	F.C.C.	1967
					A.G.M.	1968
Loder's White ***	3–4	4	white	May	A.M.	1911
					A.G.M.	1931
Moser's Maroon ***	4	4	maroon	June	A.M.	1932
Mother of Pearl ***	4	4	pink to white	May June	A.M.	1930
					A.G.M.	1968
Mrs. A. T. de la Mare ***	4	4	white, scented	May	A.M.	1958
					A.G.M.	1968
Mrs. Charles Pearson ***	4	4	bluish-mauve	May June	F.C.C.	1955
					A.G.M.	1968
Mrs. Furnival ***	4	4	light pink, blotched	May June	F.C.C.	1948
					A.G.M.	1968
Naomi	4	3–4		May		
Exbury Naomi ***			lilac/yellow		H.C.	1968
Naomi Stella Maris ****			buff/lilac		F.C.C.	1939
Nobleanum	4	3	scarlet	Dec. Apr.	A.G.M.	1926
Album ***					A.G.M.	1968
Pink Pearl ***	4	4	rose-pink	May June	F.C.C.	1900
					A.G.M.	1968
Purple Splendour ****	4	4	deep purple	June	A.M.	1931
					A.G.M.	1968
Sappho ***	4	3	white, dark blotch	May June	A.G.M.	1968
Snow Queen ***	4	4	white	May June	A.M.	1946
Tally Ho ****	3	4	scarlet	May June	F.C.C.	1933
The Master ***	4	4	shrimp pink	May	A.M.	1966

c. LOW. 4–8 feet: 1.22–2.44 m.

for near the front of borders in light woodland, to fairly sunny positions

Name	H	F	Flower colour	Time	Award	
Blue Diamond ****	4	4	blue	Apr. May	F.C.C.	1939
					A.G.M.	1968
Bo Peep ***	3	4	pale yellow	Mar. Apr.	A.M.	1937
Bow Bells ***	4	4	pink	May	A.M.	1935
Britannia ****	4	4	crimson-red	May	F.C.C.	1937
					A.G.M.	1968
C.I.S. (new)	3–4	4	creamy-yellow suffused apricot pink	May		
Christmas Cheer ***	4	4	blush pink	Feb. Apr.		
Corona ***	4	4	coral pink	May	A.M.	1911
Day Dream ***	3	4	crimson	May	A.M.	1940
Doncaster ***	4	4	scarlet-crimson	May June		
Elisabeth Hobbie ***	4	4	scarlet	Apr. May		
Elizabeth ****	3–4	4	blood red	Apr. May	F.C.C.	1943
					A.G.M.	1968
Fabia ***	3–4	4	orange-salmon	May June	A.M.	1934
Fabia Tangerine ***			orange-red			
Goldsworth Orange ****	4	4	orange	June-July	A.M.	1969
Grosclaude ***	3	4	scarlet	late May		
Jean Mary Montague ****	4	4	scarlet	late May		
May Day ****	3–4	4	scarlet	May June	A.M.	1932
					A.G.M.	1968
Moonshine (new)	4	4	yellow	May		

43

Name	H	F	Flower colour	Time	Award
Olympic Lady (new)	3–4	4	pink to white	May	
Praecox ***	4	4	rosy-purple	Mar. Apr.	A.G.M.1926
Saint Breward ***	4	4	violet-blue	Apr. May	F.C.C. 1962
Seta ****	3–4	4	white flushed pink	Mar. Apr.	F.C.C. 1960
					A.G.M.1968
Seven Stars ***	4	4	blush pink	late May	A.M. 1967
Susan ****	4	4	lavender	May	F.C.C. 1950
					A.G.M.1968
Tessa ***	4	4	rosy lilac	Mar. Apr.	A.M. 1939
					A.G.M.1968
Tortoiseshell	3	2–4	yellow to orange-scarlet	June	
Unique ***	4	4	pale ochre or yellow	Apr. May	F.C.C. 1935
Vanessa ***	4	4	pink	June	F.C.C. 1929
Vanessa Pastel ***			cream flushed		A.M. 1946
Winsome (new)	3–4	4	rosy cerise	May	A.M. 1950
Yellow Hammer ***	4	4	yellow	Mar. Apr.	

D. DWARFS. Up to 4 feet: 1.22 m.
for rock gardens and peat borders, in at least half sun

Name	H	F	Flower colour	Time	Award
Carmen ***	4	3	dark red	Apr. May	
Chikor (9 inches) ****	4	4	yellow	May	A.M. 1962
					F.C.C. 1968
Chink (3 feet) ***	4	4	greenish-yellow	Apr. May	A.M. 1961
Cilpinense ****	4	4	pink	Mar. Apr.	F.C.C. 1968
					A.G.M.1968
Curlew (1 foot) (new)	4	4	yellow	May	F.C.C. 1969
Jenny ***	3–4	4	blood red	Apr. May	
Ptarmigan ***	4	4	white	Mar. May	
Sapphire ***	4	4	blue	early May	A.M. 1967
Sarled (new)	4	3	pink to white	May June	
Songbird ***	4	4	blue-violet	Apr. May	A.M. 1957

E. TENDER HYBRIDS. Only suitable for indoors in all but the mildest sheltered western seaboard gardens or on a very protected partially shaded wall.

'Fragrantissimum' ***(H1-2: F4) the best known scented hybrid. White flowers tinged pink. Still well worth growing. F.C.C. 1868. Rather similar are 'Lady Alice Fitzwilliam' and 'Princess Alice.' 'Tyermannii' **** (H1: F4) enormous white or cream coloured lily like flowers. F.C.C. 1925.

F. AZALEODENDRONS. These are crosses between evergreen rhododendrons and deciduous azaleas. The foliage tends to be sparse and semi-evergreen. While interesting, their merit does not equal the best typical rhododendrons or azaleas. Two are given here as examples.

Broughtonii Aureum ** (H4: F3) semi-deciduous with yellow flowers. F.C.C. 1935.

Glory of Littleworth *** (H4: F4) rather striking yellow flowers with an orange blotch. Glaucous foliage. A.M. 1911.

There is also a group of hybrids, recently raised, between R. racemosum and Obtusum azaleas. These are very free flowering and quite showy. An example is:

Martine (H4: F4) mass of shell pink flowers in May; rather pale leaves.

9.4. Species Azaleas

A. DECIDUOUS

R. albrechtii H4 F3-4 (Apr. May) L1-2

In the best deep coloured forms, this is one of the loveliest of all the azaleas. Height to 10 ft. (3.05 m.). Flowers nearly flat, deep rose, pink, or light purplish rose, with olive-green spots. Winter hardy but young growth is liable to be frosted. A.G.M. 1968. F.C.C. 1962, 'Michael McLaren'.

R. atlanticum H4 F2-3 (May) L1-3

A low-growing, sometimes stoloniferous azalea with pretty tubular flowers. Height to 3 ft. (0.9 m.). Leaves up to $2\frac{1}{2}$ in. (6.3 cm.) long, often glaucous above. Flowers white or white flushed pink or purple, fragrant. A.M. 1965, 'Seaboard' white flushed pale pink.

R. calendulaceum H4 F2-4 (May June) L1-2

A wonderful azalea in the best orange or scarlet forms. Height to 15 ft. (4.57 m.). Leaves up to $3\frac{1}{2}$ in. (8.9 cm.) long. Flowers variable, yellow to orange or scarlet or salmon-pink, about 2 in. (5 cm.) across. Hardy and reliable. A.M. 1965 'Burning Light' coral red.

R. luteum (flavum or Azalea pontica) H4 F3-4 (May) L2-3

The common yellow azalea. Leaves up to 4 in. (10 cm.) long. Height to 12 ft. (3.66 m.), usually less. The flowers are very fragrant, about 2 in. (5 cm.) across. Valuable for its autumn colour. Still regarded as a garden plant of great merit. A.G.M. 1968.

R. occidentale H4 F2-4 (June Aug.) L1-2

One of the finest azaleas, especially in the carefully selected forms and strains now being introduced from western U.S.A. Height to 10 ft. (3.05 m.). Flowers up to 5 in. (12.7 cm.) across, in various shades of cream to pink, often flushed or blotched; sweetly scented. The foliage sometimes colours well. A.M. 1944, white with yellow blotch, flushed rose-pink.

R. roseum H4 F2-3 (May) L1-2

A most dainty species, with flowers of a lovely shade of clear pink in the best forms. Height occasionally to 12 ft. (3.66 m.), usually much less. Flowers tubular. Very hardy. A.M. 1955, phlox pink.

R. schlippenbachii H4 F3-4 (Apr. May) L2-3

A charming azalea with large flat-shaped flowers and nice foliage Flowers very pale pink to rose pink with reddish spots, up to $3\frac{1}{2}$ in. (8.9 cm.) across. Hardy but the young growth can be frosted. A.G.M. 1968. F.C.C. 1944 rose-pink; F.C.C. 1965, 'Prince Charming', bright rose-pink.

R. vaseyi H4 F2-4 (Apr. May) L1-2

Another first class azalea. Height to about 8 ft. (2.44 m.) but occasionally more. Flowers rose pink to white. Hardy and reliable. A.G.M. 1968. A.M. 1969 'Suva'.

B. OBTUSUM GROUP

R. indicum H2-3 F2-3 (June) L1-2

A rather tender species, only suited to the hottest and mildest parts of the country. Often low growing or prostrate. Leaves evergreen. Flowers red to scarlet or rose red, about 2½ in. (6.3 cm.) across. Useful for its late flowering. Is the parent of many hybrids including the Satsuki group. 'Balsaminaeflorum' (roseflora) a reasonably hardy low growing clone of the above with double salmon-red flowers. (F3). The "*Azalea indica*" of florists is not this species. This belongs to *R. simsii* and its hybrids.

R. kaempferi H4 F3-4 (May June) L1-2

Erect growing, often reaching over 5 ft. (1.52 m.) Leaves semi-evergreen. Flowers salmon-red, orange-red, pink to rosy scarlet. This very hardy attractive and reliable plant is the parent of many of our best hybrids, suited to cold districts. A.G.M. 1968. F.C.C. 1955 'Eastern Fire' with camellia-rose coloured flowers.

R. kiusianum H4 F1-3 (May) L1-2

An excellent hardy, low growing species, useful as a ground cover. Leaves semi-deciduous. Flowers purple, mauve, to rose-pink or rarely white. May be a parent of some of the Kurume azaleas.

R. nakaharai H4 F2-3 (June Aug.) L1-2

A first-class creeping, mat-forming dwarf. Leaves evergreen. Flowers brick-red to rose-red. A new introduction from Taiwan, with flowers produced late in the season. Seems to be quite hardy. A.M. 'Mariko' 1970.

R. poukhanense H4 F2-3 (Apr. May) L1-2

The hardiest of these azaleas. Leaves almost deciduous. Flowers rose to lilac-purple, quite large, fragrant, 2 in. (5 cm.) across. Free flowering and showy. Well worth growing in all districts.

9.5. Azalea Hybrids

A. GHENT AND RUSTICA HYBRID AZALEAS

Small flowered singles or hose-in-hose, with attractive colours and a sweet scent. June. All are F4.

Coccinea Speciosa **** brilliant orange-red. A.G.M. 1968.

Daviesii **** white flowers with a pale yellow eye. A.G.M. 1968.

Gloria Mundi *** flowers bright orange, yellow lobe.

Narcissiflora **** pale yellow double flowers. A.M. 1954, F.C.C. 1963, A.G.M. 1968.

Norma **** bright rose double flowers. A.M. 1891, A.G.M. 1968.

B. MOLLIS HYBRIDS

Large flowered with self colours. Usually sold as seedlings in mixed colours. Chiefly salmon, flame, pink, yellow and cream. All are F4.

Christopher Wren *** orange-yellow flowers.

Dr. M. Oosthoek *** deep orange-red flowers. A.M. 1920 and 1940. A.G.M. 1968.

Golden Sunlight *** ('Director Moorlands') bright golden yellow flowers.
Mrs. L. J. Endtz *** clear yellow flowers.
Spek's Orange **** orange flowers. A.M. 1948, F.C.C. 1953, A.G.M.
   1968.

C. OCCIDENTALE HYBRIDS
Fairly late flowering, comparatively large, with yellow blotch. All are F4.
Delicatissima *** flowers cream, yellow blotch, pink tinged bud, late.
Exquisita **** cream flowers, flushed pink, orange blotch, late.
Superba *** pink flowers, with apricot blotch.

D. EXBURY AND KNAPHILL HYBRID AZALEAS
Large flowered hybrids derived from the crossing of many species. They
have a wide range of colours. Often sold as seedlings, either to colour or
mixed. Nearly all are good and they are excellent value for massing. All
are hardy and are best grown in very light woodland. May-June.
Basilisk ***(F3) cream with yellow blotch. A.M. 1934.
Cracatoa (new) fiery red flowers, bronze foliage.
Firecracker ***(F4) currant-red.
George Reynolds ***(F4) buttercup-yellow, deep blotch. A.M. 1936.
Gibraltar ***(F4) orange.
Harvest Moon ***(F4) pale yellow A.M. 1953.
Lapwing ***(F4) pale yellow, tinged pink, orange blotch. A.M. 1953.
Satan ***(F4) scarlet.
Silver Slipper ****(F4) white flushed pink. A.M. 1962, F.C.C. 1963.

E. OBTUSUM HYBRID AZALEAS
Always sold as named clones.
   Kurume. Mostly fairly low growing, with a dense habit. Flowers single
or hose-in-hose, $\frac{1}{2}$-$1\frac{1}{2}$ in. (1.3-3.8 cm.) across. Early and mid May. Many
are not suitable for northern Britain where the summers are too cool to
ripen the wood. Grow in full sun or very light shade in the south and full
sun in the north where a border against a south or west wall is excellent.
Azuma-kagami ('Pink Pearl') ***(H3 F4) deep pink, hose-in-hose.
A.M. 1960. A.G.M. 1968.
Hatsugiri ***(H4 F3) purplish crimson flowers, low and compact.
   Quite hardy. A.M. 1956.
Hinodegiri ***(H3 F4) bright crimson. A.M. 1965. A.G.M. 1968.
Hinomayo ****(H4 F4) soft pink F.C.C. 1945. A.G.M. 1954.
Iro-hayama ***(H4 F3) white, margined pale lavender. A.M. 1952.
Kirin ***(H3 F4) deep rose, shaded silvery-rose, hose-in-hose. A.M.
   1952. A.G.M. 1968.
Kure-no-yuki ***(H4 F4) white flowers, hose-in-hose. A.M. 1952.
   A.G.M. 1968.
Vida Brown ***(H4 F4) rose-pink flowers, large, small bush. A.M. 1960.

Kaempferi hybrids. Taller, and more upright. Flowers single, $1\frac{1}{2}$-$2\frac{1}{2}$ in. (3.8-6.3 cm.) across. Mid to late May. These are generally better plants for northern districts than the Kurumes and flower well most seasons in a sunny position. Most have good autumn colour.

Addy Wery ***(H4 F4) bright scarlet. A.M. 1950.

Betty ***(H4 F4) orange-pink. A.M. 1940.

Fedora ****(H4 F4) dark pink. F.C.C. 1960.

John Cairns ***(H4 F4) Indian red; excellent in the north. A.M. 1940. A.G.M. 1968.

Kathleen ***(H4 F4) rosy-red. A.M. 1962. A.G.M. 1968.

Naomi ***(H4 F4) salmon-pink, late. H.C. 1964.

Willy **(H4 F3) clear pink flowers. Very hardy, excellent in the north.

E. OTHERS

Amoenum (H3-4 F2) rich magenta or rosy-purple flowers, usually hose-in-hose, small. A little tender in the north. A.G.M. 1968.

Amoenum Coccineum, unstable sport of above, light carmine-red.

Chippewa (H4 F3 New) rose-pink flowers, very late, hardy.

Everest (H3 F4 New) white, very fine large flowers.

Gaiety (H4 F4 New) large flowered pink, late May.

Galathea (H4 F3 New) brick-red flowers, unusual colour.

Maxwellii (H3-4 F3) bright rose-red flowers.

Mothers Day ***(H4 F4) red, semi-double. A.M. 1945. A.G.M. 1968.

Orange Beauty ***(H4 F4) orange-pink, A.M. 1945. A.G.M. 1968.

Mucronatum (Ledifolia Alba) ***(H4 F4) still one of the best white flowered varieties. Wrongly classed as a species. There are several varieties of this.

Palestrina ****(H3-4 F4) pure white, faint green eye. Rather tender in Scotland. A.M. 1944. F.C.C. 1967. A.G.M. 1968.

Vuyk's Rosy Red ***(H4 F4) rose-red. A.M. 1962.

Vuyk's Scarlet ****(H4 F4) deep red flowers, an excellent variety. A.M. 1959. F.C.C. 1966. A.G.M. 1968.

The Gumpo and Satsuki groups need hot sun to ripen the wood for good flower production, so are only suited to the warmest districts.

The tender indoor large flowered varieties are usually bought in flower during the winter months. There are many excellent varieties, and it is best to choose the colour that is personally preferred.

Printed in England by:

CHENEY & SONS LTD, BANBURY, OXON